AUTHENTIC
JAPANESE
GARDENS

Amidst the splendour of the scene,

and the silence,

I was filled with a wonderful peace.

Basho

Yoko Kawaguchi

AUTHENTIC
JAPANESE
GARDENS

Creating Japanese Design and Detail in the Western Garden

IMM lifestyle books

Read. Learn. Do What You Love.

For Kiyoshi and Junko Kawaguchi, and Simon Rees.

Contents

Introduction

All over the world people are attracted to Japanese gardens, usually because they provide a tranquil environment, designed to give the impression of a natural landscape at its most serene. They possess a unique aura of calm, which derives from an economical, almost minimal use of materials, whether for building or planting.

A garden in the Japanese style is intended to offer peace and quiet contemplation, with restraint, order, harmony and decorum as the guiding design principles. It is an expression of love for living things, acceptance of the transience of Nature reflected in the changing seasons, and an inspired vision of the eternal.

From the tiniest courtyards to the grandest parks, Japanese gardens invite one to linger and savour their timeless quality.

previous page: *A kasuga-style lantern stands watch over a tea-house built in a secluded dell at Tatton Park, in Cheshire.*

facing page: *Angular rocks can be dynamic; these also reflect the shape of the native fir trees which surround this dry garden designed by Terry Welch in Seattle, Washington.*

above: *Rounded mountains, lushly forested, rise up around Lake Ashi (Ashi-no-ko), forming a contrast with the austere elegance of Mount Fuji. For centuries, Japanese garden designers have sought to re-create the smooth lines and sinuous curves of the Japanese landscape. A vermilion torii gate marks the entrance to a Shinto shrine.*

Japanese-style gardens first became popular in the West in the second half of the nineteenth century. They were part of a craze for all things Japanese which swept Europe and America for about fifty years after the country first became more accessible. Until then, Japan had kept her doors tightly shut against the rest of the world with a brief exception in the seventeenth century, after which only a small group of Chinese and Dutch merchants, confined to a tiny island outside Nagasaki, were allowed to continue trading. The Dutch East India Company sent back to Europe Japanese porcelain and lacquered (japanned) chests and cabinets. What most people knew of Japan were the flowers, birds, pine trees and islands painted on these household objects.

At first, it was the idea of Chinese rather than Japanese gardens that captured the imagination of Europeans, following the well-established fashion for Chinese motifs on porcelain, furniture and fabrics. When the first western accounts of real Chinese gardens began to appear in the second quarter of the eighteenth century, they sparked off a vogue for mock-Chinese garden houses, which began in Britain and quickly spread to France and other countries. Pavilions and pagodas were used instead of classical temples, by then an established feature of English landscape gardens. In the western imagination, Chinese gardens were idyllic pleasure-grounds where languid ladies and gentlemen spent their time amusing themselves, drinking wine and playing musical instruments. When travellers returning from the Far East described real Chinese gardens as lacking the symmetry of European ones of the time (most of Europe was still under the influence of the French formal style), this apparent lack of constraint was welcomed by those eager to throw off the chains of French tradition. The charm of the Chinese style was thought to lie in the variety of scenery contained in one garden. Sir William Chambers (1723–96), the designer of the Chinese Pagoda and other buildings in Kew Gardens, felt that Lancelot "Capability" Brown (c.1716–83), the great eighteenth-century English landscape gardener, was going too far towards a "natural" style of open landscape. In his *Dissertation on Oriental Gardening* (1772), Chambers proposed a greater use of contours, a more informal and varied style of planting shrubs, especially flowering ones, and the use of buildings to add diversity to the landscape. His theories were presented as though they were the tastes of the Chinese.

Japanese gardens were also seen through a haze of preconceptions about the luxuriant, sensual East. They were considered to be as highly artificial as Chinese ones, but while Chambers believed that a careful use of artifice enhanced a garden, Japanese gardens were often described as mannered and affected. In other fields of art, Japanese styles did not produce such doubtful reactions. Once Japan began to open her doors, more screens, fans, silks and wood-block prints than ever were exported to the West, with an immediate effect on artists and other people. While painters experimented with

unfamiliar Japanese techniques, shops started catering to the taste of the British and French for exotic *objets d'art*. In 1875, Arthur Lasenby Liberty launched his first shop in London selling Japanese silks. Operas and operettas on Japanese themes were soon appearing on the stage in London and Paris, among them Camille Saint-Saëns' *La Princesse jaune* (1872) and Gilbert and Sullivan's *The Mikado* (1885). Both of these made Japan a land of fantasy, though Gilbert actually visited a Japanese village at an exhibition in Knightsbridge about the time *The Mikado* went into rehearsal. This village employed craftsmen, dancers, musicians and acrobats brought over from Japan; there was also a tea-house and a garden with serving maidens whom Gilbert photographed.

Images of Japan

The theatre had a growing pool of sources to draw on. Many travel books were published between 1870 and 1890, recording the experiences of the first intrepid visitors. Novels soon followed, often romantic tales about Japanese women and western men, set in a decadent, sensual Japan. Pierre Loti's *Madame Chrysanthème* (1887), based on his experiences as a naval officer in Nagasaki, was made into an opera by André Messager in 1893, and both forms had some influence on Giacomo Puccini when he came to compose *Madama Butterfly* (1904). Loti's central character arrives in Japan expecting to see tiny paper houses surrounded by flowers and green gardens. Though he thinks nothing of this culture, he looks forward to seeing his ideas of Japan realized, but after some time there his prejudices turn into a deep dislike for what he interprets as Japanese artificiality. Loti's novel helped to spread the image of miniature gardens with misshapen pine trees, diminutive bridges and minute waterfalls — a landscape inhabited by flitting, child-like women with butterfly sleeves, glimpsed beneath the curving eaves of a tea-house.

Another popular western image of Japan was of a land smothered in flowers. At the end of the nineteenth century, one of the greatest hits on the London stage was a musical extravaganza called *The Geisha*, which opened at Daly's Theatre in 1896. The curtains opened on a view of the Tea-house of Ten Thousand Joys, with geishas posing on a red humpback bridge spanning a carp-pond. Flowers were used to establish the "Japanese" setting: in the first act, wisteria dripped from the eaves of the tea-house (though wisteria is never grown against a house in Japan); in the second, the stage was overflowing with chrysanthemums, which flower much later (though no time was supposed to have passed between the acts). Japanese gardens were associated with a heady mixture of flowers and nubile young women. In the last act of *Madama Butterfly*, the heroine and her maid, Suzuki, dance around their house, scattering cherry-blossoms, peach-blossoms, violets, jasmine, roses, lilies, verbena and tuberoses to welcome Butterfly's American husband, Pinkerton.

Meanwhile, wealthier gardeners made it fashionable to create Japanese gardens in a corner of their estates. Japanese plants, including maples, sago palms and double-flowered kerria, had been brought to Europe late in the eighteenth century by Carl Pehr Thunberg (1743–1828), a Swedish doctor and naturalist who had travelled to Japan with the Dutch. Many more plants, among them the single-flowered kerria, many azaleas, Japanese rush (*Acorus gramineus*), the plantain lily (*Hosta plantaginea*) and the spotted laurel (*Aucuba japonica*) were introduced to Europe by Philipp Franz von Siebold (1796–1866), a German physician and naturalist who also spent some time at the Dutch East India Company trading station at Nagasaki. Both Thunberg and Siebold wrote books about Japanese plants, and both described their travels in the country. From the time of Japan's opening to the West until the outbreak of the First World War, many more plant collectors went to Japan, among them Robert Fortune (1812–80), James Gould

Veitch (1839–70) and E. H. Wilson (1876–1930) from Britain, Carl Johann Maximowicz (1827–91) from Russia and David Fairchild (1869–1954) from the United States. Fairchild is remembered in particular for his passion for flowering cherries; thanks to his enthusiasm, Japanese cherries were planted along the Potomac River in Washington, DC. In turn, Fairchild sent saplings of American flowering dogwoods to Tokyo, and these trees are still immensely popular in Japan today.

Diplomats coming home were among the first to construct Japanese gardens in Britain. A. B. Freeman-Mitford (1837–1916), who became Baron Redesdale in 1902 (and was the grandfather of the writer Nancy Mitford), was one of them. After publishing *Tales of Old Japan* (1871), he planted fifty species and varieties of hardy bamboo in his garden at Batsford Park, in Gloucestershire. His book *The Bamboo Garden* (1896) described the collection. At the turn of the century, Louis Greville (1856–1941) built a Japanese-style garden at Heale House, Wiltshire; it included a thatched tea-house and a vermilion bridge. By this time Josiah Conder's books on Japanese gardening had also appeared. An architect commissioned to design western buildings in Japan, Conder (1852–1920) wrote two studies of gardening traditions there: *The Flowers of Japan and the Art of Floral Arrangement* (1891) and *Landscape Gardening in Japan* (1893). In these books, especially the latter, readers found more bridges, stone lanterns, rocks and cropped pines to copy.

It had been known for almost a hundred years that the Chinese practised bonsai, the art of growing dwarf trees in shallow pots. An exhibit of bonsai trees was put on show in Liverpool in 1872 in honour of the Japanese ambassador and his colleagues. In the first two decades of the twentieth century, the fashion for Japanese gardening, both large-scale and in miniature, reached its peak. There was a steady trade in bonsai trees, and gardeners were brought from Japan to build

left: *Contrasting autumn colours at Batsford Park in Gloucestershire. The umbrella-shaped* Prunus hillieri *"Spire" (rear right) forms a canopy over the gazebo, while the more informally shaped* Acer rubrum *helps to blend this group into the woodland background. The vibrantly coloured* Acer palmatum *"Osakazuki" reflects the shape of the prunus, giving the group its coherence.*

below: *Japanese pines and maples are some of the most popular choices for bonsai as well as being the most important trees used in the Japanese garden.*

The idea of garden topiary is essentially the same as that of bonsai, to refine the shape of the tree to bring out its hidden beauty. The maple in this picture belongs to the var. hep-talobum *group, having the classical seven-lobed leaf form.*

gardens for wealthy patrons as Japanese gardens became the rage among the English Edwardian upper classes. The best surviving examples from the period include Tatton Park in Cheshire; Cottered, near Buntingford, Hertfordshire; and Tully, near Kildare (where another part of the estate is now the home of the Irish National Stud).

The Japanese Garden at Tatton Park, Knutsford, in Cheshire, was the brainchild of Alan de Tatton (3rd Baron Egerton of Tatton), the owner of the estate. Inspired by the visit he paid to the Anglo-Japanese Exhibition held in London in 1910, de Tatton invited a team of gardeners from Japan to lay out a garden for him. Its features included a tea-house, a Shinto shrine, a representation of Mount Fuji (with white stones to indicate its cap of snow) and a series of interflowing ponds, crisscrossed by elegant wooden bridges. The gardeners employed many Japanese plants, including azaleas, cherries, ferns and maples, to great effect. They also used various species of moss to create a verdant carpet redolent of the atmosphere of centuries-old gardens in Japan.

Coombe Wood, near Kingston, Surrey, is on the site of James Veitch's own nursery, which sold plants originally collected by Veitch himself, his son James Gould Veitch, and E. H. Wilson. The garden here still contains many of Veitch's plantings, and it has taken in the Japanese-style garden built on the estate next door, which has a particularly beautiful water garden. Of the various elements of Japanese gardens imitated in Europe, it was probably the use of water that was most easily appreciated. Ponds in naturalistic settings play an important part in the gardens created by painters as different as the Impressionist Claude Monet (1840–1926) and E. A. Hornel (1864–1933), one of the group of artists who were known as "The Glasgow Boys".

In the United States, it was the popularity of the great world fairs, hosted by cities such as Philadelphia (1876), Chicago (1893), San Francisco (1894), St Louis (1904) and San Diego (1915), which helped to disseminate knowledge of Japanese gardens and garden design. Japan was an enthusiastic participant in international events of this kind, which offered an opportunity to showcase the nation's talent, skills and achievements, both modern and traditional. A Japanese building surrounded by a garden became a familiar and popular attraction of these *fin-de-siècle* world fairs, as attested by the many contemporary postcards surviving from the era. While across America and Europe there were innumerable Japanese exhibitions (with accompanying tea-houses, gardens and "geishas") which were privately financed by western entrepreneurs, such as the one in Knightsbridge, London, attended by W.S. Gilbert, the

Japanese pavilions at the world fairs were sponsored by the Japanese government. They were showcases of authentic Japanese gardening traditions, aesthetics and taste. The materials for them, accompanied by gardeners and craftsmen, were especially exported to the United States from Japan.

A "Japanese Village" of this kind was constructed for the California Midwinter International Exposition held in 1894 in San Francisco. The driving force behind its creation was George Turner Marsh, a successful Oriental art importer. An Australian by birth, Marsh had spent some years as a young man in Japan, during which time he developed his interest in Japanese design. Marsh's ideas for the "village" were realized by the émigré Japanese landscape designer Makoto Hagiwara, who planned and superintended the construction of a garden together with a tea-house. Artisans were hired directly from Japan, and materials, including those for the garden's extraordinary "moon bridge", were assembled over there and brought to San Francisco.

After the fair ended, the site was preserved as part of the city's Golden Gate Park. Carefully managed and expanded by Hagiwara, it became San Francisco's celebrated Japanese Tea Garden. Its success inspired Marsh and other businessmen to set up their own commercial tea gardens. Such gardens became popular recreational venues for the fee-paying public. In 1921, for example, the latest spectacular attraction to open along Atlantic City's famous boardwalk was an amusement park, complete with bathhouses, a ballroom, rides, a couple of fun houses, a shooting gallery and a Japanese Tea Garden.

Landscape in miniature

The concepts underlying the Japanese art of arranging groups of rocks in the garden have perhaps been less easy to approach for western gardeners, but as an interest in eastern religions has burgeoned in the last fifty years, the esoteric aspect of Japanese gardening,

particularly the Zen Buddhist tradition, has caught the imagination of gardeners elsewhere. A group of rocks in a dry garden can symbolize Buddhist teaching, aid meditation or simply create a feeling of solidity and permanence. Though it might seem odd, there is a recognizable link between these austere, abstract gardens of

below: *This hill-and-pond garden at the Huntington Library in San Marino, California, follows the Japanese custom of creating a smooth, undulating contour to the land.*

rocks and sand and landscaped pond gardens, for if there is one thread that runs through the entire tradition of Japanese gardening during the last twelve centuries, it is a love of the diverse landscape of the Japanese islands: hills covered with pine forests and thickets of bamboo, valleys of golden rice fields, the open sea dotted with islands, the surf which rolls up on smooth, glistening sands or batters itself against a rocky coast. There is also

an affection for each of the four seasons, which are clearly marked in the temperate marine climate of the country: the snows and frost of winter, the cheerful sunshine of spring, the sheen of water on leaves during the rainy month, the relentless glare of summer, the clear blue skies of autumn.

These are the elements constantly brought into the Japanese garden. From earliest times, formal gardens represented the mountains, woodlands and waterfalls, lakes, streams and open grassland of the natural world. In contrast to the image of a bower of flowers, Japanese gardens of all styles weave their rich tapestry in shades of green, emphasized by white gravel and the greenish-grey of rocks. Flowering trees, shrubs, perennials and annuals are used with great restraint, as are plants with berries or variegated leaves. Even the use of deciduous trees, including the fabulous Japanese maples which come in such a range of brilliant leaf colours, is generally restricted. Seasonal interest is concentrated on a small number of carefully selected and positioned plants of this kind. In practical terms, this means that Japanese gardens do not have an off-season during winter, since the rocks, the sand, the trained evergreens and conifers do not change. Winter brings no dug-up borders of bare earth, simply because in these traditional gardens there are no borders or beds in the western sense.

This is not to say that the Japanese are not passionate hybridizers of plants, mesmerized like people all over the world by the endless patterns and colours Nature seems capable of throwing up in the game of genetic roulette: countless prize cultivars of tree peonies, morning glories, chrysanthemums and, more recently, calanthes have been coddled and cherished by enthusiasts. In the eighteenth century there was a craze for variegated camellias and *tachibana* oranges (*Citrus tachibana*) not unlike the tulipomania that overtook Europe in the previous century. Chrysanthemums were exhibited with just as much competitive pride as auriculas and pinks were in the north of England. These passions, however, are kept separate from the traditional art of garden-making. Fancy cultivars of *Iris ensata*, for example, are more often grown in pots than planted out in the garden, so the large, showy blooms can easily be admired much closer at hand.

Perhaps the best way of capturing the spirit of Japanese gardens is not to attempt to grow rhododendrons and maples where they simply will not thrive, or to build vermilion bridges and tea-houses — not even necessarily to create waterfalls gushing over rocks — but to try to re-create a local landscape the gardener loves. It may be done with heathers in Scotland, for example. The important thing is to draw on the means of arriving at the special stillness and serenity which Japanese gardens exude, and use them like any other garden tool, instead of trying to reproduce faithful copies of a foreign land. The aim is to achieve an effect of controlled calm by emphasizing space, austere simplicity and shapes.

Changing gardening styles

Most of the terrain of Japan has acid soil, which largely determines the choice of garden plants there. Most are native species; others, such as the tree peony, flowering peaches and flowering crabapples, were highly prized Chinese shrubs brought to Japan in ancient times; still other shrubs, like *Mahonia japonica*, were Chinese medicinal plants imported into Japan in the seventeenth and eighteenth centuries.

A handful of European and American plants have become firm favourites in Japan, especially broom and the American dogwoods. The Japanese describe their gardens as naturalistic, but they are not woodland or wild-flower gardens. Instead, a very careful selection of plants and rocks and stones encapsulates, refines and embodies the spirit of the local landscape for all to see and experience.

As more and more exotic plants arrive from overseas, garden styles are changing in Japan too. The fashion these days is for English-style gardens with lavender and old-fashioned roses, even though both tend to suffer in Japan's more humid climate. Fewer and fewer houses are being built in the traditional way with wood and wattle and daub; modern houses are made of prefabricated materials instead. Inside they have carpets, not thick straw mats; curtains, not sliding doors covered with rice-paper. For more than 1200 years, people in Japan sat on cushions on the floor; they gazed at their gardens from immaculately polished verandahs. Fifty years ago habits started to become westernized. Just as the furniture in the living-room is more likely these days to be sofas and coffee-tables, people are likely to look out on their gardens from a glass window or a patio door. Styles in both architecture and design change and develop. Gardens in Japan now tend to be brighter, with fewer sombre evergreens and more lawn. There are more flowers too. But sometimes the old ways can remind us of a different way of thinking about gardens. For those unfamiliar with the techniques and concepts traditional to Japanese gardening, learning about these traditions may stimulate new approaches and help them to realize their own visions in the gardens.

The tradition of Japanese gardening stretches back 1400 years. Though different styles developed as the social functions of gardens changed, the underlying concept has stayed surprisingly consistent. The approach has always involved paring the natural world down to its essential elements to refine an understanding of the workings of both Nature and time. Gardens are often passed on from generation to generation like prized bonsai trees. They transcend time and fashion. Their shapes and forms take on a universal appeal which brings peace to those who inherit this art of gardening.

The four basic types of Japanese gardens are described in the next chapter: hill-and-pond gardens, dry-landscape gardens, tea gardens and courtyard gardens.

facing page: *This Swiss garden seems to extend to the very horizon, bounded only by the sky and the grey silhouettes of distant mountains. The Max Koch Garden succeeds in merging flawlessly together an intimate water garden planted with* Iris laevigata *and a panoramic view over the lake. The raised decking provides an ideal viewing platform, and the choice of natural materials for both the decking and the bridge prevents them from clashing with the overall feel of the garden.*

CHAPTER ONE

Traditional Japanese Gardens

The earliest descriptions of gardens in Japan are found in seventh-century poems. From them it is possible to see that lakes and islands and bridges were already the principal features of the aristocratic gardens of that period. Picturesque rocky shorelines were also being created to add variety to the landscape.

Right from the beginning, Japanese gardens were the products of a highly self-conscious culture which tried to recreate naturalistic landscapes near people's homes, but also to find pleasure in reminders of Nature's rugged and untamed wilderness.

The hill-and-pond garden

The choice the Japanese made with regard to the kinds of landscapes they reproduced in their gardens was closely connected with how they saw their country. By building islands in the middle of lakes they were confirming their identity as an island people. Gardens of this kind came to play an even greater role in aristocratic life once the imperial court was moved to Kyoto at the end of the eighth century. As this area was blessed with many springs, as well as being watered by several clear rivers issuing from the richly forested mountain ranges surrounding the city to the north, east and west of the broad valley floor, it is hardly surprising that lakes became more significant in gardens than ever before. About the time the first imperial palace in Kyoto was being constructed, a garden was built around a sacred spring just south of the palace grounds. This garden eventually included a large lake with a sacred island, overlooked by another palace. Later aristocratic gardens in Kyoto were modelled on this imperial prototype.

For the next four centuries, a highly sophisticated culture flourished in these garden palaces. This society gave birth, for example, to *The Tale of Genji*, a portrait of the life of refined and sensitive emotions led by the nobility. Its author, Murasaki Shikibu, lived at the end of the tenth century and the beginning of the eleventh. The exquisite feelings she described include responses to the natural world, though these reactions are kept within the conventions of the time. The court revolved around a strict calendar of elaborate rituals and splendid ceremonies, and it made great formal occasions of excursions to outlying hills in the autumn. There the nobility amused themselves by picking wild flowers

which they then replanted in their gardens at home. Pilgrimages to more distant temples also provided rare opportunities for these aristocrats to leave the confines of the city. Along the way they were able to catch glimpses of white beaches, wind-tossed pines and the sea itself. These were the landscapes they wanted to have re-created for them in paintings and in their gardens.

A typical palace faced south and looked out on an open expanse of sand, a ritual space, beyond which might be some scattered planting, and then a large lake fed by a channel which was dug so that it ran into the garden from one corner of the estate, passing under several corridors of the palace on its way. This stream was embellished with rocks to simulate a rippling brook, and around it the terrain was made to undulate gently. Here, the clumps of wild flowers gathered in the hills were replanted: balloon flowers, hostas, yellow valerian

and bush clover. The inhabitants of Kyoto led their lives against the backdrop of the deeply wooded, sloping mountain ranges which hem in the city on three sides. There were also older memories of the perfectly shaped, dome-like mountains around the older capitals of Nara and Asuka – mountains immortalized in some of the oldest poetry in Japan. These "feminine" mountains are quite unlike the precipitous, craggy, dangerous

mountains lying further to the east in central Japan, those which, after the opening of the country to the West in the nineteenth century, came to be known as the Japan Alps.

The white, sparkling beaches that once surrounded the Bay of Osaka were copied in these grand gardens. For the sake of contrast, rocky shorelines were often built to represent Nature's wilder aspects. The garden

above: *A weeping willow is carefully positioned over a pond so that it casts its reflection in the water. Japanese maples are also often used in this way.*

lake would have up to three islands, all connected with bridges. During courtly entertainments, these islands provided an ideal stage for musicians, who also performed from gilded and painted boats. Guests would admire the pageantry from the palace verandah as they caught sight of the boats between the pine trees. They would listen as the music wafted closer, then became more distant as the boats floated away. Another room from which the garden could be seen was an open one built directly over the lake and connected to the rest of the palace by a long corridor. From here, or from a separate pier, elegant princes and their ladies were able to go out onto the lake themselves to gaze upon the varied scenery designed specifically to be appreciated from the water. By night, they would admire the reflection cast by a full moon on the surface of the lake.

Temple and palace gardens

Such aristocratic gardens provided the model for a type of Buddhist temple garden, which emerged in the eleventh century, built by aristocratic devotees of the Amida Buddha, an eternal Buddha believed to preside over the Pure Land in the West. The Pure Land was envisioned as a tranquil, paradisal realm dominated by a gorgeous palace overlooking a lotus pond. Here the souls of the dead were believed to sit in meditation. Temples dedicated to the Amida Buddha frequently featured a large central lake, on the far side of which stood Amida's sacred hall, from which his gilded statue cast a brilliant presence across the water.

In the twelfth century, political power began to shift to the warrior classes. Some of the most powerful of the new warlords, as well as members of the established aristocracy, became Buddhist monks in later life. They commissioned residences which were part palace, part temple, their gardens being designed for both aesthetic pleasure and spiritual contemplation. Garden features, such as arrangements of rocks, were intended to suggest

imagery belonging to Buddhist and Chinese mythology. Waterfalls assumed a symbolic significance, the rushing water representing the transience of the temporal world, against which the soul has to struggle in order to attain enlightenment, just as, according to a Chinese legend, the carp that succeeds in swimming up a waterfall is transformed into an all-powerful dragon. Paths were built to allow these gardens to be seen from different directions, and the stroll garden came into being.

The centuries of internecine warfare that followed were not conducive, however, to the construction of large-scale gardens, and it was not until peace was finally established in the seventeenth century that the stroll garden truly began to flourish. Water, buildings, rocks, moss, trees, shrubs: all had their part to play in creating the complex effect of these gardens. With the development of the tea garden in the sixteenth and seventeeth centuries, new influences were swiftly absorbed into the design of stroll gardens, and what was intimate and modest in the tea garden became grand and ambitious. It was around that time that the famous gardens belonging to the Katsura and Shugakuin Imperial Villas near Kyoto were built. At Katsura, stepping-stones, paths and bridges meander among five large and small islands. In one place, a pebbly spit of land juts out into the lake, its point adorned with a single round stone lantern standing on an outcrop of rock like a miniature lighthouse. This headland was thought to represent a celebrated landscape on the coast of the Sea of Japan, known as the Bridge to Heaven. The route around the garden at Katsura dips into shady glens and rises again towards a fanciful mountain pass, where there is a humble building like a mountain inn. As well as incorporating several landscapes in miniature, Katsura is also a tea garden, leading guests up to any one of the seven teahouses within the grounds. There are the usual features of a well-appointed tea garden: roofed benches for meeting people, stone lanterns along the pathways, and basins of water for washing hands. The palace complex

facing page: Ritsurin Park, located in the city of Takamatsu on the island of Shikoku, was the palatial retreat of the local daimyo (feudal lord). The park dates back to the seventeenth century. The rocky outcrops in the centre of the lake represent the Islands of Eternal Youth from Chinese mythology, while the building in the far distance is the elegant tea-house Kikugetsu-tei, rebuilt in 1746.

itself stands imposingly in the middle of an open expanse of lawn. With its clean, strong lines and austere simplicity, it forms another dramatic feature of the garden.

For the next two centuries, following this high point in the history of gardens in Japan, the stroll garden remained the status symbol of the highest-ranking noblemen in the country and a significant drain on their purses. It became a showcase for their aesthetic tastes, demonstrating at the same time their familiarity with classical Chinese and Japanese art and literature. Paths around the stroll garden would lead through a sequence of different landscapes, or open onto unexpected vistas, each rich in cultural associations, perhaps containing an allusion to a Chinese fable, an ancient Japanese poem, or a direct reference to a famous landscape either Chinese or Japanese. While the culture of the warrior class collapsed after Japan was forced to open her doors to the West in the middle of the nineteenth century, pond gardens continued to be the favoured style among the new social elite, although only the richest among them were able to build on a scale comparable to the lordly gardens of the past.

Man-made hills

In the West, gardeners often go to a great deal of trouble to level the ground for a smooth lawn. In Japan, manuals teach how to add contours to flat land to give added depth and perspective to a garden. If a pond or a small lake is being dug, the earth removed during its construction is ideally suited for building small mounds, hills or knolls to produce a gently undulating landscape.

How this terrain is planted up depends on the effect that is desired. The use of open spaces is a very important design element in Japanese gardens. Some gardens – especially smaller ones – are densely planted in a palette of greens in order to create the illusion of a thick woodland, but this is then frequently offset by the pond, with its smooth, uncluttered expanse of water. The planting should emphasize the beauty of the lay of the land, and this can be achieved in larger gardens by opening things up. A hillock can be embellished with a group of stones halfway up its slope, with a few azalea bushes or perhaps a sprawling juniper. Ground-cover can be varied: swathes of *Ophiopogon*, with their distinct strap-like leaves, show up well against a background of moss,

below: *Shrubs such as* Pieris japonica, *box-leaved holly (*Ilex crenata*), and azaleas can be planted among rocks to fill out awkward corners and soften their lines. Their shapes should be controlled so as to complement the rocks, not overwhelm them.*

while broad stretches of neatly trimmed, low hedging plants – azaleas or bamboo grasses – can create a pleasing contrast with open, grassy areas. Larger knolls are suitable for arrangements of taller trees. Where a garden seeks to re-create a wooded hillside, round pruned bushes and trees of differing heights can be used to produce an impression of wave upon wave of greenery.

On flatter terrain, trees of the same species can be planted to suggest the idea of a forest, but by clearing away the undergrowth, except for clumps of woodland perennials here and there to direct the eye, a sense of spaciousness can be produced at the same time. Another trick is to plant a tall shrub or tree near the principal vantage point. In Japan, a popular choice for such a position is *Osmanthus fragrans* f. *aurantiacus*, the fragrant olive, which bears clusters of intensely sweet orange flowers in the autumn. In this way, it is possible to enjoy the feeling of being surrounded by lush vegetation without actually overcrowding the garden. Using tall, top-heavy trees by themselves will naturally emphasize their height. If this threatens to overbalance the garden, the introduction of shorter but shapely shrubs, or a stone basin or lantern, will help to give more stability to the grouping.

For an artificial hill, first dig the site to the depth of 30 cm (12 in) or more in order to loosen the compacted topsoil. The earth for the mound is added in tiers 30 cm (12 in) deep, each one firmed down thoroughly before the next is added. A rod marked with the desired height of the mound will be useful in the centre, but it is a good idea to add a little extra earth since the mound will inevitably sink as it settles. The slope of the mound should be at an angle of between 35 and 45 degrees. The last step is to smooth the surface of the mound and plant it with suitable ground-cover to stabilize it.

Designing hill-and-pond gardens

The large garden: In a large garden, it may be possible to create a varied landscape with low hills, a lake, and islands linked to the rest of the garden by bridges. It is largely a question of proportion, but a lot also depends on the mood the gardener wants to achieve. To preserve a sense of open space, it might be best to have a simple island with only rocks and maybe a solitary pine tree. This will give a view of the opposite bank beyond the island, a shoreline not heavily planted but kept plain with a shingle or pebble beach. A garden that is more

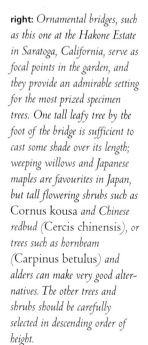

right: *Ornamental bridges, such as this one at the Hakone Estate in Saratoga, California, serve as focal points in the garden, and they provide an admirable setting for the most prized specimen trees. One tall leafy tree by the foot of the bridge is sufficient to cast some shade over its length; weeping willows and Japanese maples are favourites in Japan, but tall flowering shrubs such as* Cornus kousa *and Chinese redbud (*Cercis chinensis*), or trees such as hornbeam (*Carpinus betulus*) and alders can make very good alternatives. The other trees and shrubs should be carefully selected in descending order of height.*

densely planted would require an island that reflects the same approach, with more colour, perhaps including the use of painted bridges.

Japanese gardens work in greens, creating subtle contrasts with variations in hue, shade and tone, and also by using foliage and bark with differing textures. Evergreens, broadleaf as well as conifers, constitute the background against which the deciduous trees and shrubs, along with flowering plants, mark the passage of the seasons with their changing displays of colour. The tracery of leaves on a pruned Japanese maple looks all the more delicate when presented against the austere backdrop of a row of thick, blue-green bamboo. In bigger gardens there will be more scope for introducing trees and large shrubs which grow naturally into an elegant shape and therefore require very little pruning apart from the removal of congested branches. These can provide a foil against which to show off classically pruned trees, such as *Ternstroemia gymnanthera*, *Podocarpus macrophyllus* var. *maki* or *Taxus cuspidata*. *Kerria japonica* is graceful in its informality, with arching branches smothered in yellow blossoms in the spring-time. It serves as a wonderful background for a glossy, formally pruned camellia bush such as "Adelina Patti", with its single mottled pink flowers, or a compact, late-flowering, double-flowered cherry tree. Kerrias in

above: *Whether the garden you are designing is on a grand scale, such as this one at the temple Ninna-ji, in Kyoto, or is more modest in scope, it is important first of all to establish the overall lay of the land.*

turn can look quite stately when underplanted with *Iris japonica*, whose soft, frilly, pastel-shaded lavender flowers open around the same time.

This type of garden has something in common with the great English landscape gardens of the eighteenth century. Since the aim is to represent Nature as seen and refined through the imagination, it is better to avoid highly hybridized cultivars, especially flowering shrubs with blooms of stronger, modern colours, and also to keep plants with variegated leaves to a minimum. When strategically placed, a tree or shrub with lime-green leaves can catch the eye and introduce light to a dark corner, but too many plants with gaudily marked foliage will only diminish the effect and be distracting. This is true of bronze-leaved trees and shrubs as well. They are apt to bring autumn into the garden too early unless there is plenty of lush, green foliage around to form a contrast.

Garden design manuals dating back to the eighteenth and the early nineteenth centuries provide suggestions as to what types of tree should be selected as the key trees in a landscape garden, and also where they should be positioned. It has been traditional for the principal tree in a hill-and-pond garden to be either a pine or a kusamaki tree, *Podocarpus macrophyllus*. The principal tree is complemented by the second most significant tree in the garden, which should be a broadleaf if the principal tree is a conifer (and a conifer if the principal tree happens to be a broadleaf). It is noted in the old manuals that this second tree should be positioned near the garden pond, or on an island in the pond, and that it should be particularly graceful and help to anchor the entire design of the garden. Another important tree in a hill-and-pond garden is the one planted next to, or in front of, the garden waterfall. Its branches should drape in such a way as to partially conceal the cascading water from view. More arcane planting concepts include an evergreen for the eastern end of a south-facing garden to catch the rays of the morning sun, paired with a deciduous tree for the western end so that the rays of the setting sun might filter through its branches.

A Japanese-style garden of this sort would not be difficult to integrate into a larger, western-type landscape garden. While fences and hedges play an important role in other Japanese styles, stroll gardens have such a degree of affinity with landscape gardening generally that a wall separating a Japanese area from the rest of the garden might actually seem an unnecessary barrier. The attraction of a Japanese garden is its sense of being a special place, and a garden in any kind of foreign style is going to be special by virtue of its own difference. This special place does not have to be defined by a wall. The secret to creating a successful Japanese garden within a larger scheme lies in the choice of the site: perhaps a secluded out-of-the-way dell, where a mysterious pond might be just right. A toad-stool-shaped lantern of natural, uncut stone can help to signpost the area. On the other hand, all expectations can be confounded by boldly letting a spacious vista open out where the visitor least expects it. Japan is a densely forested country with many swift streams and tranquil mountain pools. It is this intimate presence of Nature which Japanese gardens try to capture.

Japanese gardens are designed to be viewed from specific vantage points. There may, of course, be more than one vantage point in a single garden. If the garden has a path, there will be specific spots along the way from which different views of the garden can be appreciated. These spots are usually indicated by some kind of garden feature that prompts visitors to stop, draw breath and take a look around. The most obvious is a bench or a gazebo, but it can be a stone lantern or something as simple as a stepping-stone wide enough to stand on with both feet. A judiciously positioned tree set along a garden path—*Stachyurus praecox*, which produces tiny flowers on long racemes resembling dangling strings of minute beads, is a good example—

facing page: Selaginella kraussiana *makes a good alternative to moss, and since it belongs to the fern family, it goes well with other members of that group of plants. They thrive in areas with high humidity where they produce lush growth. The rock protruding from the surface of the pond is of a type often used in Japan because it is thought to resemble a carp raising its head out of the water.*

will induce people to stop and admire, not just the tree, but also a wider view of the garden.

All over the world people are attracted to Japanese styles of gardening because they produce a sense of tranquillity, even of spirituality. The effect is seldom attributable simply to the use of particular religious imagery, whether it be statues of Buddha or a *torii*, the gate made of a horizontal beam and a lintel supported on two pillars, which serves as the gateway to a Shinto shrine. It is more often a cumulative effect of the design of the entire garden. The key to the Japanese idea of spirituality is this sense of a sacred space, a space which is separate and distinct from the mundane, everyday realm of existence. An island in the middle of a lake can become a sacred space; so can a dry-landscape, stone-and-sand garden and even a tea garden. But this special space can also occur in the middle of a commercial building in the form of an indoor garden – or in a back garden, through the use of fencing. By shutting out the external world, a garden can both help to concentrate and enlarge the mind. This idea of a sacred space is not particularly foreign to the West. Sacred trees, rocks and wells are found all over Europe, and sacred spaces act as a focus for the awe which Nature as a whole can inspire in us.

A *torii* gate usually marks out the sacred precincts of a Shinto shrine. The propriety of putting *torii* gates in western gardens is perhaps questionable; even from the sole consideration of proportion and harmony in the garden, a full-sized *torii* gate actually needs a shrine building to counterbalance its somewhat ponderous presence. It is after all a gate, and gates lead somewhere, but an island in a lake could be given an inconspicuous, smaller *torii* gate to indicate its sacred status. An acceptable alternative is a small household shrine; many traditional Japanese gardens used to include these shrines, which were no more than about 90 cm (3 ft) or so high, with a small vermilion *torii* in front of them. But it cannot be emphasized enough that these shrines

are objects of worship. The same can be said for statues of Buddha. Stones engraved with a bodhisattva, a holy spirit, are often found by ancient roads in Japan. These, too, are objects of veneration and are usually tended affectionately by local people.

The smaller garden: In a small garden, it might be too ambitious to have both a pond and hills, but there are several alternatives which draw upon the various traditional styles of gardening. One option is to dedicate most of the garden to a large pond, preferably a shallow one, surrounded by very low ground-cover – moss or *Ophiopogon*, varied with liriope or ferns; several low-growing, shade-tolerant shrubs with berries, such as *Ardisia japonica*, *Aucuba japonica*, or the taller *Osmanthus heterophyllus*; and then a few trees with their lower branches carefully removed. The trees will then form a delightful canopy. A different feeling altogether is achieved when the surrounding banks of the pond are planted quite densely with round, pruned azalea bushes, interspersed with a few maples, clipped pines and rocks, maybe with a lantern. This kind of planting is even more effective if the ground rises towards the back of the garden, conveying the impression of a wooded hillside.

Experiment with different levels of planting in the garden. The contrast of texture between low ground-cover and a broad swathe of clipped shrubs, for example azaleas, *Sasa veitchii* (bamboo grass) or *Photinia glabra* (an evergreen with attractive red leaf-buds), that continues down the far side of a mound can be very attractive. Another effective technique for creating a feeling of depth is to plant a tree on the far side of a slope, so that only part of it is visible from the house. This will help to create an illusion that there is more to the garden, tucked away out of sight. The technique of partly hiding garden features – whether it is a tree, a waterfall or a stone lantern – is very important in Japanese gardens. It not only creates a sense of distance in a smaller garden, but it encourages the visitors to the

facing page: *The atmosphere of a mountain retreat is created by this rustic gateway and the simplest style of bamboo fencing, the* yotsume, *which lines the entrance pathway. The contrasting colours and textures of the gravel, the chipped bark, moss and the black-leaved* Ophiopogon planiscapus *"Nigrescens" produce an agreeable sense of formality and quiet dignity here at the Bloedel Reserve in Washington State.*

garden to use their imagination. A tree or shrub that is half-glimpsed is considered extremely attractive. If the garden is too densely planted with many different kinds of perennials and shrubs, this effect will be lost.

Sloping ground can be combined with a meandering brook toward the bottom end of the garden, along with some trees. This will leave a patch of open ground nearer the house, which can be embellished with stepping stones, a lantern or rocks; or clumps of ferns, a *Fatsia japonica*, or low-growing shrubs. Perennials such as astilbe, with its frothy pink plumes that contrast so well with the dark green leaves, and *Filipendula purpurea*, which also form attractive clumps with feathery flowers, are ideal for planting next to small streams. Around limpid pools and basins of water, choose the delicate nodding flowers of *Begonia grandis* subsp. *evansiana*.

Traditional houses in Japan invariably possessed a wide verandah which was separated from the neighbouring rooms by sliding doors fitted with paper screens. The garden could be enjoyed either from the verandah or, when the sliding doors were fully open, from the rooms inside, when the entire breadth of the garden could be seen. A similar effect can be achieved with a glass wall, which can diminish the sense of a barrier existing between house and garden. One way of capturing the feel of a verandah is to build a wooden terrace or deck above the level of the rest of the garden. Japanese houses are still raised off the ground in order to keep the woodwork properly aired during the humid summers. Traditionally, a large stone was placed near the verandah to serve as a step down into the garden. Wooden steps can serve a similar purpose. A terrace of this kind would also provide a space for entertaining, which traditional Japanese gardens lack.

right: *The sliding doors of a room open to reveal a hill-and-pond garden in this city residence belonging to the Iwasa family, one of the priestly families serving the ancient Kamigamo Shrine in Kyoto.*

Ponds, streams and rills can be constructed close to a house provided that they pose no threat to the foundations of the building. Since Japanese houses are traditionally built with the floors raised 45 cm (18 inches) off the ground, it is possible to look out over the pond from inside the room.

Pruned azaleas, box-leaved holly (Ilex crenata) and rocks fill in the space in the foreground, allowing the eye to descend gradually to the level of the pond. The bank at the back of the garden rises steeply and a rock is strategically positioned so it will be at eye-level when seen from the room, producing an illusion of depth and distance.

Plants for different situations

Planting along the back of the perimeter of a large garden: *Sciadopitys verticillata, Torreya nucifera, Lithocarpus edulis.*

Chief specimen tree: *Pinus densiflora, P. parviflora, P. thunbergii, Podocarpus macrophyllus, Ilex integra, Chamaecyparis pisifera* "Plumosa", *Sciadopitys verticillata, Chamaecyparis obtusa* var. *breviramea, Taxus cuspidata, Ternstroemia gymnanthera,* Japanese maples, *Lagerstroemia indica, Prunus mume.*

Specimen tree for planting on or around the back of a mound or hillock: *Quercus myrsinifolia, Q. serrata,* Japanese maples, pines, *Podocarpus macrophyllus* (yew pine), *Diospyros kaki* (Japanese persimmon), *Chamaecyparis obtusa* var. *breviramea, Ilex crenata* (box-leaved holly), *I. integra, Taxus cuspidata* var. *nana* (Japanese yew), *Ternstroemia gymnanthera, Sciadopitys verticillata* (Japanese umbrella pine), *Magnolia grandiflora.*

Accompaniment for specimen trees or on islands in the middle of ponds: *Pinus parviflora* (Japanese white pine), *Ilex crenata* (box-leaved holly), *Taxus cuspidata* var. *nana* (Japanese yew), *Ilex integra,* Japanese maples, *Magnolia stellata, Cornus kousa, Euonymus oxyphyllus, Enkianthus* spp, azaleas.

At the foot of specimen trees: Evergreen azaleas, satsuki azaleas, *Ardisia crenata, A. crispa, A. japonica, Euonymus japonicus, Osmanthus heterophyllus, Arbutus unedo* "Compacta", *Pieris japonica, Farfugium japonicum.*

At the foot of garden stones: *Aspidistra elatior, Liriope muscari, Ophiopogon japonicus, Hosta* spp., *Rohdea japonica,* ferns, *Ardisia crenata, Sarcandra glabra, Saxifraga fortunei, S. stolonifera, Platycodon grandiflorus, Taxus cuspidata* var. *nana.*

Underplanting for deciduous trees: *Ophiopogon japonicus, Erythronium japonicum* (Japanese trout-lily), *Tricyrtis hirta* (toad lily), *Epimedium grandiflorum, Syneilesis palmata, Aspidistra elatior, Chloranthus japonicus, C. serratus, Heloniopsis orientalis, Clintonia udensis, Disporum smilacinum, Liriope muscari, Calanthe discolor, Iris japonica.*

Weeping trees for the pond-side: pines, *Podocarpus macrophyllus* (yew pine), *Acer palmatum* and cultivars, *Juniperus chinensis, Taxus cuspidata* var. *nana* (Japanese yew), weeping cultivars of willow and cherry.

By ponds and lakes: *Albizia julibrissin* (silk tree), Japanese maples, *Taxus cuspidata* var. *nana, Ilex serrata* (Japanese winterberry), *Juniperus chinensis, Hydrangea* spp., *Malus floribunda* (Japanese crab), a wisteria pergola, *Disanthus cercidifolius*, satsuki azaleas, *Corylopsis pauciflora* (buttercup witch hazel), *Rhododendron reticulatum* and other spp., *Callicarpa japonica* (Japanese beauty-berry), *Spiraea thunbergii;* "wild" flowers: *Reineckea carnea, Cypripedium japonicum* (lady's slipper), *Equisetum hyemale* (scouring rush, horsetail), *Iris laevigata, Saururus chinensis, Begonia grandis* subsp. *evansiana.*

In front of a waterfall: evergreens, Japanese maples, weeping willow.

Above a waterfall: live oaks, *Osmanthus fragrans* f. *aurantiacus* (fragrant olive), *Ilex integra*, evergreens (but not conifers).

Downstream: *Acorus gramineus* (Japanese rush), *Pieris japonica* (Japanese andromeda), *Equisetum hyemale* (horsetail), *Eurya japonica, Iris ensata, I. laevigata.*

To prevent erosion of earth around streams and ponds: *Acorus gramineus* (Japanese rush).

By a bridge: weeping willow, Japanese maples.

For the east end of a south-facing garden: evergreens with beautiful foliage such as pines, *Cryptomeria japonica* (Japanese cedar), *Ternstroemia gymnanthera.*

For the west end of a south-facing garden: deciduous trees such as Japanese maples, flowering cherries, *Prunus mume* (Japanese apricot).

On an embankment: *Juniperus chinensis, Lespedeza* spp., *Spiraea cantoniensis* (Reeves's spiraea), azaleas, *Ophiopogon japonicus.*

Among trees planted on a slope: bamboo grasses such as *Sasa veitchii* and *Shibataea kumasaca, Hydrangea* spp., azaleas, *Begonia grandis* subsp. *evansiana, Iris japonica.*

Shrubs for planting en masse: (formally pruned) azaleas, *Camellia japonica, Taxus cuspidata* var. *nana;* (informal) *Spiraea japonica, S. thunbergii, Lespedeza bicolor, Hydrangea* spp., *Hypericum patulum, Mahonia japonica.*

Next to a gazebo: shady trees such as tall Japanese maples, *Diospyros kaki* (Japanese persimmon), *Castanea crenata* (sweet chestnut).

Shrubs and shorter trees for the front of the garden: satsuki azaleas, *Enkianthus* spp, *Ilex serrata, Prunus mume, Nandina domestica, Daphne odora, Corylopsis pauciflora, C. spicata, Osmanthus fragrans* f. *aurantiacus, Loropetalum chinense.*

Near the garden gate: *Torreya nucifera, Ilex integra, Ternstroemia gymnanthera, Ginkgo biloba.*

facing page: *Aristocratic palaces in eleventh-century Kyoto possessed rooms built over the garden lake. This garden creates a similar effect with decking, which forms a viewing platform over the water. The pond is not actually very large, but the use of tall shrubs at the far end of the pool creates the illusion of depth.*

The dry-landscape garden

In the fourteenth century, Buddhist monks, including some very eminent Zen priests, were already involved in designing temple gardens with groups of dry rocks representing various Zen concepts and Buddhist imagery. These early clusters of rocks stood on the gently undulating slopes of hill-and-pond gardens. Unlike the more austere stone-and-sand gardens of later periods, these gardens were not completely dry but often still contained ponds or springs and were lush and green. Even though the rocks were symbolic, it was never-theless important that they should look as if they had naturally come to rest where they lay.

Dry rock gardens grew in popularity, especially among temples which were not so well supplied with water, until in the seventeenth century there was a reform of temple regulations, and the south garden, which faced the central hall of the abbot's residence, fell out of use for important religious rituals. These areas were transformed into flat dry gardens featuring the white sand or gravel with which they had origi-nally been covered. These new gardens sometimes included moss, shrubs and pine trees, but they had no water. The mountains and rivers which had always been components of traditional gardens were now represented in abstract and motionless forms — in groups of rocks suggesting waterfalls, and sand swept into patterns which stylized the appearance of currents. The idea of representing flowing water with raked gravel suited the discipline of Zen sects, for the abstract shapes helped to exercise the mind, and the gardens became an aid to meditation on time,

right: *Native American firs provide a backdrop for this dry-landscape garden at the Japanese Garden in Portland, Oregon. It is edged in the traditional manner with round azaleas. The fine white gravel is raked to suggest ripples of water, while a flat rock reinforces the illusion that the expanse of sand is a lake.*

facing page: *The Japanese Garden in Bad Langensalza, in central Germany, was opened to the public in 2003. This dry waterfall landscape follows closely in the footsteps of tradi-tional Japanese garden design. The stones have been arranged to represent a series of cataracts and cascades flowing down from distant mountains. A stone bridge crosses the river (repre-sented by the raked gravel) at the foot of the cascades.*

eternity, transience and permanence.

Laid out on flat, rectangular areas, often clearly demarcated (and separated from the outer world) by a fence, a mud wall or a tall hedge, these gardens pursued the ideal of arresting movement in stillness — of capturing what is timeless in this mundane, transient world of ours. Meant to be viewed from the verandah of the monastery building, these gardens were not casual constructions. No one descends into them except to sweep them. Extending the full length of the abbot's hall, they were designed so that when all the sliding doors were drawn back, they formed an integral part of the priest's quarters. In some instances, the abbot's hall was surrounded by such gardens on more than one side.

Notwithstanding the presence of great expanses of fine, sparkling gravel, Japanese dry-landscape gardens are not dry in the sense that they are arid, and

the plants chosen for these spaces, restricted in number though they may be, are not necessarily drought-tolerant. On the contrary, they are frequently the very opposite, exemplified by moisture-loving moss, which makes such a distinctive contribution to the design of these gardens. In some temple gardens, the moss has been allowed to take over a substantial area, but so long as the garden landscape contains no running water, and the

presence of the traditional pond and garden stream are symbolically represented, these gardens are still considered to be "dry". This is yet another example of how gardens of this type succeed in merging contradictory concepts together.

In order to create the impression of spaciousness in what are frequently quite confined spaces, garden stones play a central role in these gardens. Not only are they employed to represent vast waterfalls, but

next page: *Dry-landscape gardens can be adapted to fit the smallest spaces, with green areas planted to simulate shorelines and islands. Keep the planting to a minimum; suitable trees include Japanese maples, pines, and Stewartia pseudocamellia, often planted in Zen temple gardens. For still smaller gardens, foliage plants, ferns, azaleas and shorter bamboos are good choices.*

they frequently represent islands floating in the restless ocean currents (symbolised by the stillness of the raked gravel), or the summits of gargantuan mountains emerging up out of an ever-swirling sea of mist. Trees and shrubs planted in these gardens tend to be very tightly pruned to set off the shape and beauty of the stones. There are famous gardens in which ancient camellias, grown tall over the centuries, have been planted behind a stone intended to represent a waterfall and clipped so as to represent a range of mountains soaring behind that distant sheet of imaginary water. In other gardens, the slope rising behind, and forming a backdrop to, the dry landscape itself has been planted with azaleas, carefully pruned to suggest rounded cumulus clouds overlooking the earth with its seas and islands.

Daisen-in, a subsidiary temple of Daitoku-ji, a Zen Buddhist temple in Kyoto, possesses one of the most elaborate symbolic rock gardens. The rocks are arranged to represent a dry waterfall tumbling down the side of a vast mountain. At the bottom, a bridge of rock spans a craggy gorge. A narrow mountain stream, represented by a band of sand, winds its tourtuous way among the rocks until it eventually broadens into a wide river on which a boat-shaped stone sails. On one side of the waterfall stand two tall boulders, representing a ridge of mountains. These are not the gentle mountains of Japan, but the jagged, precipitous mountains depicted in Chinese scroll paintings of the Sung period (960–1279). This style of painting became well-known and popular in Japan, especially among Zen Buddhist priests for whom calligraphy was both an important discipline and an art form. At the same time, the rock on the right is identified with Fudo-myoo, Acala in Sanskrit, the Buddhist god of fire, the punisher of all evil, while the one on the left is identified with Kannon, the bodhisattva of mercy. As this temple belongs to a Zen sect of Buddhism, there is

also a low, flat-topped boulder representing a seat used by a priest practising meditation. The garden also contains groups of rocks representing a turtle and a crane, both auspicious creatures in Chinese Taoist mythology, which was introduced to Japan in the fourth to fifth centuries. Fifteen turtles were believed to support a Mountain of Eternal Youth, where holy sages who had attained everlasting life flew on the backs of cranes.

above: *The garden at the Zen Buddhist temple Raikyu-ji, in Okayama prefecture, Japan, is said to have been designed around 1604 by the famous garden designer and tea master Kobori Enshu. The gravel symbolises the vast ocean, while the banks of pruned azaleas represent surging waves. The triangular rock is shaped like the outstretched wing of the auspicious crane, and represents Mt Horai, the principal Isle of Eternal Youth.*

Some gardens became less and less representative or symbolic, and increasingly austere and abstract, finally eliminating everything except sand, rocks and a little moss. Ryoan-ji Temple in Kyoto is the best known example of this type. This garden is 10 m (33 ft) deep and 25 m (82 ft) wide, and consists of fifteen rocks altogether, arranged in five groups: one group of five rocks, two of two rocks and two groups of three. Although water is suggested by patterns raked in the sand, the interpretation of the groups of rocks is ultimately left to the viewer. The rock garden at Ryoan-ji is deceptively simple; it is a garden that does not give up its secrets easily, for it is executed in the most abstract and esoteric of all styles of Japanese gardening. Gardens of this type depend absolutely on the quality – the beauty and the form – of each individual stone.

Designing a dry-landscape garden

Dry-landscape gardens do not necessarily have to be flat. Groups of rocks can be situated on "islands" in the sand; these "islands" can consist of mounds of earth stabilized with moss or *Ophiopogon*. A larger mound, often in the form of a turtle island with a leaning rock representing the turtle's head and neck, can be planted with a pine tree, the tree of sages, its banks indicated by more stones. Islands in a sea of sand can be suggested not only in this way by the use of rocks, but also with closely pruned, rounded shrubs such as azaleas and the dwarf Japanese yew, *Taxus cuspidata* var. *nana*.

A stream or river-bed of pebbles can help to add interesting contours to the dry-landscape garden. When the pebbles are laid out so that they slightly overlap each other like the scales of a fish, they can cleverly suggest the flow of the current. Choose the pebbles carefully for their colour and sheen. Slabs of rock can serve as bridges over these imaginary brooks.

Larger areas of land can be represented by solidly planted bamboo grass, box-leaved holly, or *Photinia glabra*, cropped low. Wild flowers too can be incorporated into the garden design, growing in small clumps on islands of moss (*Farfugium japonicum*, the balloon flower *Platycodon grandiflorus*, and *Ardisia crenata*, with its crimson berries, are favourite Japanese choices for this role), but smaller Japanese gardens tend to be very minimalist in the number of different plants they use. The basic tone of green in a garden is varied through the use of plants with different textures – springy moss and leathery-leaved camellias, for instance – and through the imaginative placing of clipped shrubs.

An area of white gravel can form a startling contrast with a swathe of moss or low, clipped bamboo grass, but the two areas can be made to harmonize with each other if the line of division is made sinuous rather than straight and harsh. This is particularly effective in gardens which are not flat but undulating. Short trees and shrubs, trimmed into a hedge either high or low, are commonly used in all types of Japanese gardens as a kind of screen that partly conceals a section of the garden from view. Low partition fences and sleeve fences are used for a similar purpose in the smallest gardens, including dry ones.

In dry-landscape gardens, the ground-cover – whether it is moss or *Ophiopogon*, or even thyme or chamomile – must make a distinct contrast with the sand or gravel areas. This means that the sand or gravel must be kept clean and not allowed to get muddy or green and slimy with algae. Hosing down the sand and raking it afresh is part of the regular cleansing ritual of a Zen Buddhist temple. It is admittedly easier to keep sand clean in a hot climate than in a wet, cold one, but the effort is what counts.

facing page: *The gravel used in dry-landscape gardens does not have to be white, although it is more challenging to create a contrast of light and darkness using gravel of more sombre colours.*

This rooftop garden in New York, designed by Jeff Mendoza, is based on a theme of cool grey-blues and bright greens. In the corner a Japanese white pine with blue-green needles links the two thematic colours together.

above: *Large flat foundation stones from ruined temple buildings were treasured and lovingly reused in dry-landscape gardens and tea gardens. One of these circular stones in a Zen temple garden serves as an image of perfection and wholeness, while also acting as a reminder of the faith of past generations and of the passage of time. Here at Silverstream in Weybridge, two stones have been used for a similar effect, their smoothness forming a contrast with the jagged upright rocks. The con-centric circles raked into the gravel around them suggest calmness and order emanating from the centre of the universe.*

Plants in a dry-landscape garden

Dry-landscape gardens need not be devoid of colour. Shrubs and trees as diverse as camellias, tree peonies, *Prunus mume* (Japanese apricot), flowering cherries, *Stewartia monadelpha* and crape myrtle can be successfully introduced. Azaleas in spring add a note of vibrancy to a garden with their range of soft pinks through to magenta-purples. Nevertheless, avoid choosing many different kinds of shrubs which flower at the same time. Too many clashing colours can be distracting, like an embarrassment of riches. Against a backdrop of evergreens, introduce one or two deciduous or flowering trees or shrubs to evoke the feeling of the evolving seasons. Appreciate how they change from day to day, from month to month. A similar effect can be produced with a careful selection of one or more perennials in well-defined clumps: the fiery orange of double-flowered day lilies, *Hemerocallis fulva*, or the purple balloon flower, *Platycodon grandiflorus*.

Choose the accent plants with conviction, for they make a statement about what the gardener feels about the season – the intensity of summer heat or the calm regrets of autumn.

The care of moss

Moss is guaranteed to grow in the middle of your prized lawn, but it will stubbornly refuse to appear where the gardener wants it to thrive. Moss dislikes direct sunlight, preferring the more gentle light of morning or dappled shade. It also requires moisture. In Kyoto, where the most famous moss gardens are found, late afternoon showers are not unusual through spring and summer. In areas where the weather cannot be relied upon to provide this essential moisture, it is a good idea to give the moss a very light watering in the early evening. Try to avoid using tap water directly, for it contains harsh chemicals and minerals. Allow it to stand for two or three days before using it. Although moss needs moisture, it will not grow in ground which is saturated with water. The soil should be free-draining, and preferably sandy. Shady trees, bamboos and hedges in a moss garden help to block the wind which can dry the air. Moss should be protected from frost by covering it with pine needles or straw. This winter protection can become an appealing garden feature in its own right.

Other plants for the dry-landscape garden and the moss garden

Wide single hedges or tall ground-cover: *Cleyera japonica, Eurya japonica,* azaleas, *Shibataea kumasaca*.

Specimen trees: *Pinus parviflora, P. thunbergii, Ternstroemia gymnanthera, Juniperus chinensis, Podocarpus macrophyllus, Chamaecyparis obtusa* var. *breviramea, Taxus cuspidata, Ilex crenata, Lagerstroemia indica,* Japanese maples, *Cycas revoluta, Stewartia pseudocamellia.*

above: *A bare crape myrtle stands guard at one end of the stone bridge in this dry-landscape garden. Crape myrtle is grown in Japanese gardens for their beautiful bark and their elegant shape, as much as for their lovely flowers. A striking Sago palm (Cycas revoluta) leads the eye deeper into the garden.*

Tall hedges: *Lithocarpus edulis, Quercus glauca, Q. myrsinifolia, Viburnum odoratissimum, V. suspensum, Photinia glabra, P. x fraseri, Eurya japonica, Euonymus japonicus.*

"Wild" flowers: spring: *Iris japonica;* summer: *Hemerocallis* spp. (day lilies); late summer: *Astilbe* spp., *Platycodon grandiflorus* (balloon flower), *Tricyrtis hirta* (toad lily); autumn: Japanese anemones, *Farfugium japonicum, Aster tartaricus, Liriope muscari, Physalis alkekengi* (Chinese lantern, winter cherry).

Bamboos and grasses: *Tetragonocalamus quadrangularis, Phyllostachys nigra, P. sulphurea; Miscanthus sinensis* (eulalia, Chinese silvergrass).

Ground-cover: *Ophiopogon japonicus, Sedum kamtschaticum.*

Shrubs: *Eurya japonica, Citrus tachibana* (tachibana orange), *Juniperus chinensis* var. *procumbens, J. conferta,* satsuki azaleas, *Enkianthus perulatus, Camellia japonica* (common camellia), *C. sasanqua,* flowering cherries, *Prunus mume* (Japanese apricot), *Forsythia suspensa, Rhododendron japonicum, R. quinquefolium, R. reticulatum,* azaleas, *Cornus kousa, Lagerstroemia indica, Lespedeza* spp. (Japanese bush clover).

By a large plant pot: *Pieris japonica, Euonymus hamiltonianus* subsp. *sieboldianus, Taxus cuspidata* var. *nana* (Japanese yew), *Torreya nucifera* (Japanese nutmeg yew), *Ilex serrata, Aspidistra elatior, Farfugium japonicum, Iris japonica.*

above: *The Portland Japanese Garden, in Portland, Oregon, incorporates different Japanese garden styles, including the* hira-niwa *("flat garden"). A* hira-niwa *is distinguished by the absence of the two most common elements of traditional Japanese gardens: a dug pond and raised knolls. Many* hira-niwa *are designed as dry-landscape gardens, but dry-landscape gardens do not necessarily have to be a* hira-niwa, *as they can possess a dug pond, although this pond remains unfilled with water. Here, the moss represents a gourd-shaped island and the white gravel, the ocean.*

facing page: *This square lantern with no shaft is an example of an oki-gata lantern. A very traditional, contoured, moss-covered, Japanese garden is combined very successfully here with a European country-style roofed wall.*

The tea garden

The Japanese tea ceremony had its inception in the fifteenth century as a social entertainment devised by the Zen monk Murata Juko, who was under the patronage of the shogun, the overlord of the entire country, Ashikaga Yoshimasa (1436–90). A stylized ritual of preparing and drinking green tea with one's guests, it was quickly elevated to an art form through the genius of a succession of disciples, most notably by Sen-no-Rikyu in the sixteenth century, who championed the aesthetic principles of *wabi* and *sabi*, which involved simplicity, tranquillity, solitude and the dignity of age. In a time of great civil upheaval, Rikyu became a tea master to two of the most powerful and charismatic warlords of the period in succession. In the battle of wills on which he embarked with the second of them, Toyotomi Hideyoshi (1537–98), who had succeeded in subjugating the whole of feudal, war-torn Japan under his rule, Rikyu was to stamp his own strong personality on the tea ceremony forever. His preference for humble, rustic, weathered surroundings for his tea ceremonies was a direct challenge to Hideyoshi's love of ostentatious displays of power and wealth – he travelled with a personal tea set made of gold. Rikyu modelled his tea-rooms on the traditional image of the forest hermitage, the thatched single-room retreats of Buddhist hermits who had eschewed the world. The sole surviving example of his tea-rooms is barely more than 1.8 m² (6 ft²) in size, the walls made of straw mixed with cow dung. Although close to other temple buildings, it is reached only through the garden. Guests were expected to lay aside their swords and sit side by side, soldier and merchant, in mutual enjoyment of tranquillity and tea.

Rikyu believed that the garden, laid out as an approach to the tea-room or tea-house, had an important part to play in preparing guests for the tea ceremony. He laid stepping-stones, and for light, set up stone lanterns, something which until then had primarily been associated with temples and shrines. He also brought in the use of stone basins, low ones, moreover, which required guests to crouch in order to handle the bamboo scoop with which they could pour water to rinse their hands. Each of these features was designed with some purpose in mind to help guests purify themselves, in both body and soul, in readiness for the enjoyment of tea. This type of garden is generally known in Japanese as a "passage-way" garden (*roji*).

Under the Tokugawa Shogunate, which ruled Japan from 1603 to 1867, the formal tea ceremony continued to serve an important social function

above: *A Japanese effect can be produced using local materials instead of bamboo. A simple Western-style wooden fence is combined here with a gateway of Japanese design (Riverwood, Portland, Oregon).*

among the ruling classes. Feudal lords incorporated tea-houses (often more than one) into the design of their hill-and-pond stroll gardens. This was the style of garden which nineteenth-century visitors to Japan chiefly encountered, and helps to explain why, in the West, the image of the Japanese tea garden became so closely associated with pond gardens (another reason may well have been the fact that Japanese restaurants and places of refreshment, which were referred to as "tea-houses", although the formal tea ceremony did not constitute a part of their business, often possessed a picturesque pond garden). But even in the context of these landscaped hill-and-pond stroll gardens, the tea-houses usually possessed an adjoining *roji*-style tea garden, sometimes nothing more than a small courtyard with stepping stones, a lantern and a low water basin, but separated from the rest of the park by a fence and a gate of some kind. The Japanese term for "tea garden", *chaniwa* or *chatei*, is usually used to refer to a *roji* garden.

A *roji* garden is traditionally divided into two sections—the outer and the inner garden—each separated from the other by a hedge or a fence, and a gate. A covered shelter with benches provided with round, woven seat-mats is usually situated in the outer garden for waiting guests. Here they are able to pause and meet each other before going forward to greet their host. Passing through the inner gate, they

facing page: *In this garden, designed by Marc Peter Keane, granite slabs and millstones are combined to create a path leading up to the inconspicuous entrance to a tea-house. A slightly raised, flat stone acts as a step up to the tiny porch. The projecting cedar bark sleeve fence to the right partly conceals the tea-house from view.*

left: *A flat piece of granite makes a good bench, for instance, one to be placed under a wisteria pergola. Here it can be seen that the stone is not given a high polish, though wood is often varnished to bring out the beauty of its grain.*

leave behind the chaotic bustle of worldly existence. Hence, in some tea gardens this inner gate is nothing more than a square opening cut into a mud wall; the guests must crouch in order to pass through it. But the inner gate can also be simple and rustic, constructed of roughly hewn timber and logs, with or without a gabled roof of thatch or shingles. A gate of this kind is meant to create the impression of a forest retreat. The urban tea garden seeks to re-create a deep forest setting in the city.

The tea garden is made more enjoyable by subtly changing the mood between the outer and the inner garden. The outer garden can be bolder in design, perhaps with larger stepping-stones, or a formal six-sided *kasuga*-style stone lantern. Alternatively, it can be given rocks with contrasting shapes, textures and colours, and in this way can be made more abstract than the inner garden. The planting scheme should also be subtly different in the two main divisions of the garden. The inner garden can be planted up to suggest a type of forest, pine or maple, for example. But this is not to say that these gardens are like the naturalistic woodland gardens of the West. A select number of plants creates the illusion of many. The variety of different kinds of plants is carefully restricted to the bare minimum necessary to produce the desired image of sylvan solitude. Trees, shrubs and clumps of ferns or grasses are juxtaposed with each other seemingly without any order or sense — they are not arranged according to height, nor do they form anything resembling a border or an island

left: *Classic examples of tiny courtyard gardens are found in central Kyoto, where houses and shops jostle together along narrow, grid-like streets.*

Light filters down into this garden, which belongs to Ichi-riki-tei, an old tea-house restaurant. There is a well with *a bamboo cover and a small shrine. The lanterns give a sense of shape to the yard. The planting is severely restricted to evergreens, which have a calming effect on the eye. The shape of each tree and shrub is very well defined.*

bed. Rikyu himself preferred the trees and shrubs in his tea gardens not to be tightly clipped into shape, but at most lightly pruned so as to bring out their natural beauty and grace. The ground-cover of moss, liriope or *Ophiopogon*, or even a patchwork of these, is subtly arranged to suggest a forest undergrowth through which stepping-stones pick a path around groups of shrubs and clumps of ferns. The ground-cover comes right up to the base of the plants. Never are many different shrubs thrown together in one

daringly placed rocks and lanterns so that they could only be seen from the tea-house window. Once the guest enters the special space of the tea-room, the garden is left behind with the rest of the world. Just as the tea ceremony focuses on what is immediate, each stepping-stone, which carefully measures the speed with which guests stroll through the garden, helps them attune themselves to the present moment.

The tea garden is, above all, a functional space. The principle behind it is to have everything immac-

left: *This example of a traditional layout for a water basin is in Monaco. The basin is placed on a rock in the middle of a pebble-lined sink, or "ocean" as it is referred to in Japanese. The boulder to the right of the basin is intended to hold a basin of hot water. An added feeling of privacy is provided by the koetsuji-style sleeve fence.*

mass. The basic idea, common to all the different kinds of Japanese gardens, is that each plant in the garden should be capable of being appreciated for its own shape and form — not necessarily from a single angle. The meandering track of stepping-stones helps produce unexpected perspectives and surprises.

The tea garden is not intended to be looked at from the tea-room, although a few early tea masters

ulately prepared so that guests can be welcomed hospitably, naturally, and seemingly effortlessly. There might be tiny bridges consisting of a single slab of stone to help suggest a forest rill. A low stone basin suggests a cool mountain spring or brook, by which guests need to crouch in order to refresh themselves, washing their hands and rinsing their mouths just as people do at shrines and temples.

Many traditional basins are stoups hewn out of a piece of natural rock. In former times, a piece of carved stone rescued from the ruins of a temple or salvaged from a wrecked lantern was sometimes reshaped as a basin, a practice encouraged by Rikyu himself; similarly, old disused lanterns from shrines or temples were used in tea gardens before tea masters began designing their own. A more geometrically regular, round basin, based on the design of a coin, or a square one with bas reliefs of Buddha carved into its sides, suggests a rustic well-head.

Just as the guests purify themselves with water, the host cleanses his garden with water before their arrival. The idea of purification takes its most stylized form in the "ornamental" privy found in the inner garden of the most traditional tea gardens. This is usually a simple room arranged with rocks and sand. It is not intended for use; like much else in the tea garden, the functional is turned into a work of art.

Nor is anything that looks ornamental actually superfluous. Tea gardens are intimate, not grand. They make a virtue of the tight, awkward spaces tucked around the side of buildings. Since modesty is considered a virtue in a host in Japan, the beauty of the tea garden comes from the cumulative effect of the simple and natural materials used for its fittings. Sen-no-Rikyu sought beauty in natural forms — for example, in the rocks he chose for his stepping-stones and basins. The three Sen schools of tea in Japan, each tracing its descent from one of Sen-no-Rikyu's grandsons, still faithfully preserve his tradition of the tea ceremony.

Another of Sen-no-Rikyu's own disciples took a different approach, however. Rather than trying to make gardens appear natural, Furuta Oribe (1543– 1615) and his disciple, Kobori Enshu (1579–1647), sought to draw attention to their art. Oribe developed a style distinct from Rikyu's by deliberately introducing the artificial, the man-made, into his gardens. He set out to startle, to confound expectations, to draw attention to the artificiality of gardens. He defied convention by positioning his lanterns so that they tilted slightly, a hazardous thing to do in a country prone to earthquakes. He even transplanted towering dead trees into his gardens, and placed them so that they could not be ignored by his guests. He and Enshu both experimented with geometrical designs, using cut stone for paths instead of restricting themselves, like Rikyu, to naturally shaped stone. Even when it came to natural stone, Oribe sought out large rocks which split flawlessly along a seam so that they gave the impression of having been artificially cut. Whereas Rikyu had striven to exclude anything from the garden that attracted special attention to itself, Oribe and Enshu went so far as to emphasize design over function.

Characteristically, the Oribe school of tea came to be associated with a specific design of lantern which still bears his name. While Oribe himself appears not to have restricted himself to any one design, his disciples eventually did, principally in order to establish their own individual style, distinguishing them from all the other various schools of tea, with which they were in hot competition for students and followers. Early tea masters had used discarded votive lanterns from old temples and shrines, but the *oribe* lantern did away with the base and was intended to be stuck into the ground. It also departed from traditional styles in having a distinctive round bulge below the lantern cage. Many historians believe that the figure usually found carved on the shaft of early examples of this type of lantern came to be associated with Christ by Japanese converts to Christianity, and that these vaguely cross-shaped lanterns became their disguised objects of worship after Christianity was proscribed throughout the country in 1613.

Strictly speaking, a *roji* is a tea garden only if it is

intended for the use of the participants of a tea ceremony. Put another way, a garden is a tea garden no matter how simple it is, so long as it serves the functions of one, which is to prepare the guests for the ritual of tea-drinking. But even if you are not a tea master, the tea garden offers a distinct approach to the whole idea of gardening: rather than being a landscape to be admired, the tea garden can be appreciated only by walking through it a single step at a time — it is a series of constantly changing tableaux which cannot all be seen at once. It is also an enclosed space separated from the outside world by tall hedges, a traditional mud wall or a perimeter fence of closely-woven bamboo or of bamboo and cedar bark. In this sense, a tea garden condenses within a much smaller space the pleasures of a larger stroll garden. The difference is that the tea garden has a single purpose, which is to guide guests to a specific place. It is important that the expectations of your guests should not be disappointed, that the tea garden should lead somewhere special, whether it is a pergola, a gazebo or a summer-house.

Designing a tea garden

A point to keep in mind when designing a tea garden is that you do not want your guests to rush through it. The main gate into the garden needs to be carefully positioned, and plants strategically placed around it, so that the ultimate destination — the tea-house itself — is not in full view from the entrance. The garden should be allowed to unfold its own surprises. It is important, for example, that the bench in the outer garden should not give guests a view of their host bustling around with last-minute preparations in an adjoining area of the garden, for this would completely destroy any sense of occasion. A guest must not be harried into washing his or her hands by a conspicuously placed stone basin — it should be slightly hidden behind some greenery, or a

short partition fence. A way of encouraging guests to take time in each part of the garden is to screen off parts of the next section. Many of the most celebrated tea gardens have more than one path, each leading into different areas of the garden, which are marked off by hedges or bamboo fences. The secret of designing a tea garden is to incorporate these features without creating a sense of clutter. The challenge is to make a small area seem more spacious than it really is.

Gravel, paths and plants

When designing a tea garden, put to one side the idea that perennials and shrubs have to be confined to beds. In a sense, a *roji* garden is one big bed, with paths running through it. Gravel or ground-cover plants can be used to mark out different sections of a garden, without the need of fences or hedges. Enshu created patterns in his gardens by covering wide sections of them with beautifully coloured pebbles and leaving the rest bare and mossy. There he planted his few choice trees: *Prunus mume* (Japanese apricot), Japanese maples and pines. His stepping-stones boldly crossed both areas. Paths also have the effect of dividing a garden space into sections. The challenge is to integrate the paths into the overall design of the garden. A broad path can split a garden apart into halves; thus there has been a tendency to avoid them in many types of Japanese gardens, unless it is a path leading up to a formal gate. Stepping-stones, on the other hand, can help a gravelly area to blend and merge seamlessly into an area devoted to moss. Ground-cover, moreover, does not have to consist of a single type of plant — this is not a lawn. It can be moss with tussocks of *Ophiopogon* or liriope, or it can be liriope varied with tufts of fern. This sort of mixed planting is more difficult with grass turf, which is occasionally encountered in Japanese gardens nevertheless.

left: *This courtyard garden, belonging to the Ban family in central Kyoto, is planted in the manner of a tea garden. Horse-tail (*Equisetum hyemale*) forms a short screen around the water basin, while the scattered planting of Japanese maple, Japanese apricot and* Cleyera japonica *allows glimpses of a partly hidden stone lantern.*

Tea gardens are different from other types of Japanese gardens in that man-made hills, waterfalls and formally arranged groups of rocks do not play a major role in them. Instead, it is the planting which determines the feel of the garden. Space being at a premium, the effect is produced not by a mass of closely planted vegetation, but by the shapes of carefully chosen specimen trees and bushes. Although shrubs like azaleas can be pruned into neat, round spheres, most plants are chosen for the gracefulness of their natural forms. Pruning is therefore more a question of tidying up – removing crossed, crowded or weak branches. The pleasures of Japanese gardens are those of Nature: her shapes, colours, and textures. Abstract shapes tend to be less important in a tea garden than in dry-landscape temple gardens. Oribe and Enshu, however, as we have seen, took a different approach. In the end, each school of tea has its own cherished traditions, but these precepts should guide, not stifle, the imagination.

Traditionally speaking, the most important thing when it comes to planting a tea garden is to meet the needs of the tea ceremony. The use of plants has always been an important way of controlling the amount of light which filters into the quiet preserve of the tea-room. Light that is too bright is considered distracting. It can be frankly uncomfortable. On the other hand, a room that is gloomy or damp can also be disagreeable. In countries where sunlight is weak during the winter months, it is probably a good idea to have deciduous trees near the room instead of the more traditional evergreens. This will let in whatever light is available. There has always been a tendency in Japan to prefer the privacy provided by

evergreens, particularly conifers. This was Sen-no-Rikyu's own choice. He excluded everything in the garden which could distract attention away from the flower arranged in his tea-room. Rikyu is said to have dug up his entire patch of summer morning glories so that a single perfect bloom might be displayed for his patron Hideyoshi.

Oribe and Enshu introduced more diversity into the tea garden, although they too were sparing in the use of flowering and fruiting trees and shrubs. Even now, shrubs bearing small, pale flowers in shades of white or lavender are considered the most suitable for the subdued elegance of a tea garden: these include the more refined lacecap hydrangeas, sasanqua camellias and enkianthuses. Witch hazels have a pleasing tree shape and graceful yellow or orange ribbon-like flowers in late winter. Like any of the various Japanese maples available of differing leaf shapes and colour, witch hazels can serve as a brilliant herald of the approach of autumn. Rikyu swept his tea gardens many hours before he expected his guests: any brightly coloured leaves which fell afterwards he allowed to remain where they were on the moss. Oribe, on the other hand, chose only reddened dry pine needles to scatter under all his trees, whether they were conifers or not. Enshu went a step further and arranged the drifts of pine needles on his moss.

In Japan, flower petals—cherries, Japanese apricots and camellias—are often allowed to lie where they fall, since they scatter before they discolour, and they carpet the moss with their beautiful hues. Cherries, however, tend not to be planted in tea gardens as they are thought to be rather showy, although more types of flowering shrubs are considered acceptable now than in former times. Nonetheless, it is traditional to avoid shrubs which have stridently coloured flowers, as well as unusual or curious plants which draw special attention to them-selves. Also shunned are flowers like the gardenia, which have an overpowering scent. Since *roji* gardens tend to be narrow, any vigorous or bushy plants will cause problems by quickly overgrowing their allotted space. It is therefore advisable to keep branches trimmed and out of the way of the path. Moss is often grown between stepping stones so that guests will not slip on wet leaves or grass.

If space is very limited, a sense of openness can be created by reducing the amount of underplanting, and choosing short ground-covering plants like moss and *Ophiopogon* to go under the specimen trees. Hostas, *Farfugium japonicum* and *Aspidistra elatior*, with their architectural leaves, can look striking if they are not overcrowded and swamped by other plants. Treat them, as well as shrubs such as *Daphniphyllum macropodum* and *Dendropanax trifidus*, as you would specimen trees: allow each plant just enough space for it to be admired properly. It is surprising how a feeling of spaciousness can be created simply by clearing away clutter at ground level. Dead wood and suckers need to be removed from shrubs, as well as such twiggy growth and awkward, straggly shoots as are produced, especially towards the base of a plant. Reduce the number of main stems on shrubs which look too densely packed. In order to emphasize the height of the taller trees, their lower branches too should be taken off, leaving a clean, smooth trunk.

Naturally, there will be appropriate places for visitors to pause as they walk along the path — where there is a gate, for instance, or a bench, or a fork in the path, marked by a stepping-stone larger than the rest. Other significant spots around the garden include stone basins and the actual door of the tea-house from which your guest will go back into the garden. All of these will be the principal vantage points from which the garden will be seen. Position the most important garden features with this in mind. A specimen tree, such as *Torreya nucifera* (Japanese nutmeg yew), *Ilex integra*, *Ternstroemia gymnanthera* or *Ginkgo biloba* (maidenhair tree), is sometimes planted near the gate for the guests to admire as they leave the garden. Another tradition has been to plant a large

pine behind the tea-house so it can be seen above the roofline and add depth to the garden.

Plants for a tea garden

Hedging: *Cleyera japonica, Euonymus japonicus.*

Ground-cover: mosses, ferns, *Ophiopogon japonicus, Pachysandra terminalis.*

Main tree: *Pinus densiflora, P. parviflora, P. thunbergii, Sciadopitys verticillata, Podocarpus macrophyllus, Ternstroemia gymnanthera.*

Shrubs: (evergreen) *Dendropanax trifidus, Mahonia japonica, Pieris japonica, Eurya japonica, Taxus cuspidata* var. *nana, Ardisia japonica, A. crispa, A. crenata,* bamboos; (deciduous) *Helwingia japonica, Ilex serrata, Lindera* spp.

Flowering shrubs: *Enkianthus perulatus, Hydrangea paniculata, Rhaphiolepis umbellata, Rhododendron quinquefolium, Styrax japonicus, Exochorda racemosa, Camellia japonica, C. sasanqua.*

Around a basin: *Nandina domestica, Pieris japonica, Eurya japonica, Aucuba japonica, Ilex serrata, Taxus cuspidata* var. *nana,* ferns, *Equisetum hyemale.*

Behind or near stone lanterns: pruned pines, *Ilex crenata, I. integra, Sorbus commixta, Ternstroemeria gymnanthera, Torreya nucifera.*

Near the front of a stone lantern: Japanese maples, *Ilex serrata.*

"Wild" flowers: *Saxifraga stolonifera, Disporum smilacinum, Polygonatum falcatum, Platycodon grandiflorus, Tricyrtis hirta, Calanthe discolor, Chloranthus japonicus, C. serratus, Chelonopsis moschata.*

facing page: *This water basin is situated in a fairly public, open area of the Japanese Garden near Portland, Oregon. The pruned mugo pine to the right and a slightly shorter Japanese maple to the left provide a feeling of height to the overall arrangement and, along with the neatly clipped hedge and the large rock in the foreground, subtly produce a sense of place.*

The courtyard garden

The hill-and-pond garden, the dry-landscape garden and the tea garden are the three historical branches of the Japanese tradition in gardening. However, in practical terms, the buildings — the merchants' and artisans' houses, the shops, inns and restaurants — that formed the heart of the ancient city of Kyoto, that epicentre of the art of Japanese gardening, were, and still are, very cramped for space. With perhaps only a room or two facing onto the street, these buildings are narrow and long. And as you pass along their maze-like succession of rooms, you will come across tiny, square, courtyard gardens, wells of greenery surrounded on all sides by rooms and corridors.

The smallest of these courtyard gardens are called *tsubo-niwa*, a *tsubo* being the basic square measure used in Japan for calculating space — it equals 3.3 m² (36 ft²).

right: *The tiniest rectangular gardens (such as this one belonging to the tea-house Ichiriki-tei, in the Gion district of Kyoto) are intended to be viewed from inside a room by a person sitting on a cushion on the floor. Hospitality and welcome are implied by the water basin and scoop.*

A short sleeve fence in the teppo *style (see also page 128) partly screens the left corner of the garden. This type of fence allows glimpses of what is beyond it, and the half-seen* Pieris japonica *creates the illusion that the garden extends much further in that direction.*

above: *Decking here creates a raised corridor from which the courtyard garden can be viewed. The corridor allows a close-up view of the fine* Pieris japonica *and the bronze-leafed maple. The shallow end of the pool is laid with pebbles, and the planting, consisting of marginals such as rushes and water irises, is arranged in groups among the rocks to provide areas of clear water on which the maple can cast its reflection.*

These gardens are very private, meant to be seen up close, often in passing, as people go about their daily business, or by those sitting in one or another of the adjacent rooms.

If the garden is open on all sides to various rooms and corridors, it needs to be designed so it can be appreciated from all angles. In one of the traditional entertainment quarters of the ancient city of Kanazawa, there is a old tea-house (now a museum) with an enclosed courtyard garden serving several purposes. The kitchen of the establishment, as well as the private living quarters of the proprietress, looks out onto this tiny well of a garden, which brings light, air and the welcome sight of some greenery to these cramped ground-floor rooms. At the same time, the garden has been designed with stone lanterns, so that when lit, the garden could be appreciated in the gathering dusk by the patrons of the tea-house as they were being entertained by geishas in the reception rooms upstairs.

Courtyard gardens can be very shady, occupying as they do those tricky little spaces in and around, as well as between, buildings. In the built-up areas of Kyoto, not much light manages to find its way into many of these minuscule gardens, though they are open to the elements and catch the rain. These gardens are often ideal for that beloved component of all Japanese gardens, moss. Where moss refuses to oblige and thrive, *Ophiopogon* can be used instead for ground-cover. Other shade-tolerant plants, like *Aucuba japonica* (spotted laurel) and *Fatsia japonica*, are chosen to complement perhaps a moss-grown stone lantern or a stone basin. These would not be meant for actual use, although a lantern could be lit sometimes, and usually several handsome stepping-stones will also be laid across the tiny space. Admittedly, these gardens can look somewhat sombre, particularly if they are planted with ever-greens. Yet that slightly musty smell of leaf-mould

facing page: *A lantern is sometimes placed on the far shore of a pond or lake to focus the eye. Larger ponds demand a tall* kasuga *lantern rather than this smaller* oribe *lantern, which is right for this intimate courtyard garden designed by Paul Fleming. In place of a lantern, an expansive hill-and-pond stroll garden might have a group of rocks representing a waterfall.*

above: *This is an example of a tall stone water basin, intended for use from the verandah if the room for the tea ceremony was located in the house. Horsetail (Equisetum hyemale) is very popular in Japan for planting around water basins. This arrangement is by Marc Peter Keane, the American garden designer and writer who lives and works in Kyoto.*

left: *This garden by Marc Peter Keane incorporates a western-style patio and water feature. The eaves of the house extend out to form a pergola, up which vines have been planted.* Akebia quinata *and* Stauntonia hexaphylla *are both fruiting climbers used for pergolas. The leaning tree in the foreground is supported in the traditional Japanese manner against a horizontal piece of timber.*

that blends so naturally with the scent of the wood of which traditional houses were built characterizes Japan. Modern commercial and municipal buildings which employ a lot of glass often manage to produce a more airy feeling to their courtyard gardens than the wood, wattle and daub, and tiled-roof construction of traditional Japanese city dwellings. One way to brighten an enclosed courtyard garden is to use fine gravel to create, if not an elaborate dry-land-

scape garden with arrangements of garden stones, a simple garden with bamboo, for instance, instead. The fine gravel can be raked into patterns. The Imperial Palace at Kyoto has gardens of this kind, laid out with clean white gravel, in each of which only one kind of shrub is grown: wisteria, bamboo, or Japanese bush clover.

When designing a tiny courtyard garden, as with any other kind of garden, it is necessary to keep in mind how and from where it is to be seen. Since Japanese houses are always raised above ground level, a tall rock may not seem as impressive to a person who is standing up as it would to somebody sitting on a cushion on the floor in the traditional Japanese fashion. On the other hand, if a tiny garden is to be viewed from a standing position, a very flat stone can be effective against a background of white gravel. A very low ground-cover plant like *Liriope muscari*, with its elegant leaves and pale flower spikes, can appear insignificant if it can only be seen from above and from a great height. Partition fences woven of bamboo, or using other kinds of grasses or even bark, can be used to separate off areas even in the smallest gardens. These sleeve fences do not extend all the way across the garden, but serve as a sort of rustic screen. For instance, they help to make a doorway more sheltered, and they add to the tiniest gardens that element of partial concealment and surprise which has always been important in Japanese garden design.

Trees with a gracefully branching habit, like maples and witch hazels, will draw attention to the horizontal. They can be planted for contrast next to a slender tree such as a small, carefully pruned pine tree. Tall, slender plants like bamboos and pines will emphasize height, especially if their lower branches are meticulously removed and they are not cluttered with underplanting. The juxtaposition of the tall with the short will create a sense of spaciousness even in small gardens.

A shade-tolerant daphne, like *Daphne odora*, will turn a tiny courtyard garden into a well of scent in early spring. Japanese gardens do not have an off-season, for they are on show all year round. This is why evergreens play such an important role. Green is undoubtedly the dominant colour of Japanese gardens. The pleasure of winter comes from waking to find frost patterns on the leaves of *Aucuba japonica* (spotted laurel), or a mound of snow perched on a

left: *The slender trunks of these maples become a feature of this courtyard garden in their own right. The eye is drawn to the verdure of the underplanting: the soft mosses, the leathery aspidistra, and the delicate fronds of the ferns. In the middle of the garden water trickles from a bamboo spout into a small pool, suggesting a natural spring. This garden was designed by Paul Sheppard.*

facing page: *A glass roof lets plenty of bright Australian sunlight into this pond garden in Melbourne. The island in the centre of the pond is connected by a stone-slab bridge to the Japanese-style verandah.*

stone lantern. This will give some idea of the importance of the initial choice and layout of the various components of the garden. Herbaceous plants do not substantially change the look and feel of traditional Japanese gardens during the spring and the summer months as they do in western gardens with mixed borders and beds. Plants need to be chosen for their year-round interest — for the shape of their individual leaves, for the gracefulness of their branches and for their overall shape. This is especially the case in an intimate enclosed garden. It would be sad if such a garden was allowed to fall into neglect; it would be a constant reminder and reproach — an embarrassing, cluttered cupboard that is always open.

The courtyard garden can look back to any of the other traditional types of gardens. Moss and white gravel can be arranged to represent an island in the ocean. The moss can surround a rock or a choice shrub. The gardener might decide to model a courtyard garden on the most austere style of dry-

below: *A yukimi-style lantern is commonly used alongside water as in this Californian courtyard garden.*

landscape garden, with sand and rocks and no plants. A bed of pebbles can be made to represent a meandering stream, with a miniature stone lantern indicating a headland jutting out into symbolic water. A lantern next to a stone basin refers back to the graceful hospitality of the tea garden.

This is the most flexible type of garden, which does not have to be restricted to inner courtyards of old houses. Miniature gardens of this kind can make use of any confined or awkward strip of enclosed space around the house. The smallest and narrowest garden can be created in the space available outside a ground-floor window. It can be embellished with a lantern, a basin or a rock, raked white gravel, *Ophiopogon*, or a single specimen of *Nandina domestica*. In place of a garden designed to be looked down onto from the window, a different approach would be to choose, for example, a tree with a graceful habit and interesting bark so as to compose a picture, as it were, which is then "framed" by the window itself. Consider putting up a bamboo fence or a hedge to conceal elements of the view which you feel mars the composition of your "picture", such as a bleak concrete wall or an air-conditioning unit. In former times, gardens built alongside traditional Japanese houses were frequently designed to be chiefly viewed from inside the dimly-lit rooms, with the sliding *shoji* doors drawn open, so that the dark wooden floorboards of the verandah, the long horizontal transom and the vertical posts framed the bright view of the garden outside, making it resemble an unfurled scroll painting.

One way of utilizing a long and narrow urban back garden surrounded by high fencing or walls is to make a virtue of the sense of privacy it already possesses. The garden can be divided into two parts, informally indicated by a low, open-weave bamboo fence. The outer area of the garden can be used to indulge a passion for a wide range of plants. The inner garden then becomes the sanctum, an uncluttered refuge with a stone lantern and a basin, or a haven with a single pool of water. It will thus become a restful place of reflection, contemplation and peace.

Plants

As in tea gardens, it is a good idea in warm climates to give this type of garden a good sprinkling of water before the arrival of guests so that the plants and rocks do not look hot and dusty but cool, fresh and gently inviting.

Aspidistra elatior is excellent for moist, shady sites. Smaller *Acer palmatum* cultivars, as well as camellias, both of which appreciate partial shade and protection from cold winds, can do well in courtyard gardens (but beware of frost in colder climates). More unusual plants seen in Japanese courtyard gardens include the hardy Japanese banana *Musa basjoo*, though this requires full sun.

Plants growing in courtyard gardens need to be tidied and neatly pruned so they do not outgrow their allotted space. All dead branches and old, tattered foliage should be removed. It is unwise to plant very vigorous, tall-growing trees, but medium-sized and small trees can be kept manageable by stopping their central leader when they reach their desired height and thinning the number of side branches. This applies also to bamboo.

Bamboos, which can quickly become invasive out in the open (most bamboos native to Japan are of this type), may be easier to contain in courtyard gardens. Nonetheless, use specialist root barriers to prevent the spreading rhizomes damaging buildings. Remove superfluous culms to avoid overcrowding. Older culms that are more than two or three years old should be cut back to ground level. New shoots will then emerge in the spring, or in the autumn, in the case of winter-shooting varieties of the *Chimonobambusa* group. When bamboo is planted in Japan, they

left: *A gateway opens into a courtyard dominated by a monolithic rock feature with a cascade. The sliding glass doors with which the courtyard is surrounded help to keep this garden bright and prevent the central feature from becoming too oppressive. More time is needed for the planting to grow into the right shapes and sizes to become an integral part of the design.*

are often set out in three, five or seven distinct clumps, since these are considered to be auspicious numbers in Japan.

Traditional plants for the courtyard garden

Specimen plants: *Musa basjoo* (Japanese banana), *Cycas revoluta* (Japanese sago palm), *Fatsia japonica*, bamboos, *Nandina domestica*, *Camellia japonica*, *C. sasanqua*, *Stewartia pseudocamellia*, *Enkianthus* spp., *Lindera* spp., *Mahonia japonica*.

For underplanting: *Iris japonica*, *Liriope muscari*, *Ophiopogon japonicus*, *Saxifraga stolonifera*, *Aspidistra elatior*, *Hakonechloa macra* "Aureola", *Ardisia crispa*, *A. crenata*.

For ground-cover: *Ophiopogon japonicus*, *Reineckea carnea*, *Sasa* spp., *Ardisia japonica*.

"Wild" flowers near a plant-pot: *Equisetum hyemale* (horsetail), *Ardisia japonica*, *Saxifraga stolonifera*, *Rohdea japonica*, *Bletilla striata*.

For a rock garden: *Hepatica* spp., *Matteuccia struthiopteris* (ostrich fern), gentians, *Selaginella tamariscina*, *Rohdea japonica*, *Platycodon grandiflorus* (balloon flower), *Reineckea carnea*, *Bletilla striata*, *Tricyrtis hirta* (toad lily), *Ardisia japonica*, *Commelina communis*, *Aquilegia* spp. (columbines), *Physalis alkekengi* (Chinese lantern), *Eupatorium japonicum*.

CHAPTER TWO

The Elements of a Japanese Garden

The features that go into the composition of a Japanese garden all have their part to play in the creation of a single serene and harmonious landscape. Although western eyes may at first be confounded by the formality of the pruning and the abstraction of the groupings of rocks, the Japanese have always characterized their various garden styles as naturalistic, for each in its own way seeks to represent a vision of Nature that is calming, contemplative and beautiful.

Plants

There is at least one subtle difference between gardens in the West and traditional Japanese ones; though it is not often pointed out, it is absolutely fundamental. The Japanese do not confine shrubs and perennials to beds. You will not find that familiar feature of western gardens – the contrast between the open, even sweep of a well-manicured lawn and the riot of colours and textures confined to herbaceous borders and beds. Japanese gardens contrive to create an impression of luxuriance without actually using a great many plants. Individual trees or shrubs are carefully positioned so that they suggest the presence of a whole thicket, or even a forest. Each plant is chosen for its shape. Pruning therefore becomes a very important task, the principle being to bring out the inherent shapeliness of the plant by careful trimming and removing awkwardly placed, overcrowded branches.

For all shrubs and trees, it is important to clear away weak or dead wood and remove congested branches, downward-pointing growth and long, non-flowering spurs. Suckers, which sap energy from the plant and may also be growing from the root-stock if the plant has been grafted, should also be cut out.

Shaping plants

Perhaps shrubs and trees are trained and pruned harder in Japan than western taste allows. Nonetheless, pruned plants play an important part in the overall design, for their sinuous outlines give rhythm and movement to the Japanese garden. Pruning is believed to have become an important aspect of Japanese

gardens from the fourteenth century onwards.

The basic idea is to observe and respect the inherent shape of a plant. Many trees helpfully give us clues to the shapes hidden within them. There are conical conifers such as the sawara cypress, *Sciadopitys verticillata* (Japanese umbrella pine) and *Juniperus chinensis* "Kaizuka". Trees of this type need hardly any pruning at all to keep their shape. *Dendropanax trifidus* and *Daphniphyllum macropodum*, both of them useful evergreens, are likewise popular for their fine shapes. Japanese maples, witch hazels and deciduous azaleas, such as *Rhododendron quinquefolium*, *R. reticulatum* and *R. japonicum*, have naturally delicate, branching forms. Still, they all require basic maintenance and attention. Dead, weak and diseased branches need to be cut out to allow new growth.

right: *Judicious and careful pruning has brought out the naturally graceful sweep of the branches of this pine tree.*

previous page: *A sudden spell of cold weather late in the autumn produces the best colour in Japanese maples, which can be breathtaking. One of the most reliable and popular of the autumnal red-leaved maples is "Osakazuki" (Moon of Osaka). Let the leaves rest for a while where they have fallen, for they produce drifts of colour on the ground. Flowering Japanese cherries shed their petals in a similarly decorative way.*

When buying trees and shrubs, it is important to look for young plants which have the potential to grow into the shapes needed in the garden. For example, a *Daphne odora* sapling which is already leggy will be difficult to prune into a globe. Some *Ilex integra*, *Osmanthus heterophyllus* (holly olive) and yew saplings will be suitable for growing into bushy domes; other young plants of the same species may have strong central trunks, which will make them

good subjects for more elaborate topiary.

Ilex crenata (box-leaved holly), *Podocarpus macrophyllus* (yew pine) and *Ternstroemia gymnanthera* can all be trimmed into beautiful domes. So can garden camellias. *Ilex crenata* is also a good hedging plant, along with *Taxus cuspidata* var. *nana* (Japanese yew) and semi-evergreen azaleas. These low-growing shrubs are often clipped into neat globes, and are important in Japanese gardens as they are used to "anchor" a

above: *In Japan, formally pruned trees and shrubs are often used in a woodland setting to create a feeling of order amidst nature's profusion. Here, an umbrella-shaped dwarf Japanese yew (*Taxus cuspidata*) echoes the shape of the stone cap on the adjacent lantern.*

Japanese topiary

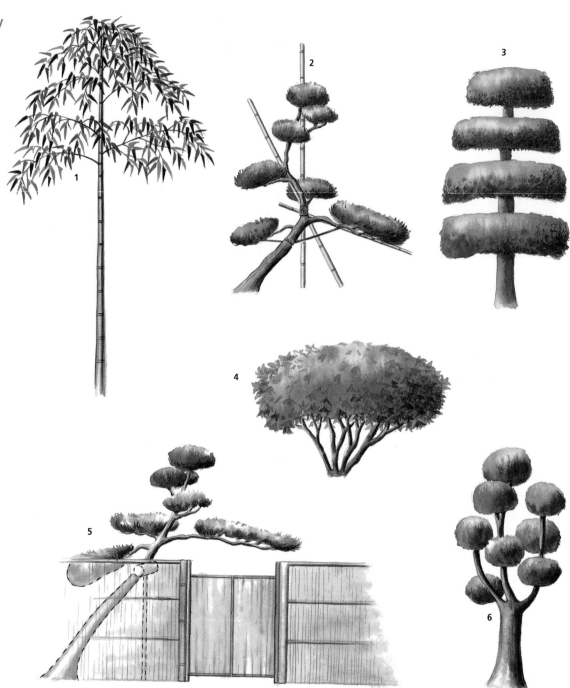

1 *Bamboos grown in the garden often have their lower branches removed to emphasize height. When they are evenly dotted around a garden, they form a cool canopy of leaves.* Sinobambusa tootsik *is a popular choice in Japan for this treatment. Specimen bamboos grown in large plant pots can retain some of their lower branches, but they should be evenly spaced along the central stem.*

2 *A curved trunk on pines is made by supporting the tree with stout bamboo canes, which are also used to train large branches on pines, yews, and box-leaved holly. To create an open tree shape, branches are pulled downwards and fastened with rope to the tree trunk. Any stems growing along the underside of the branches are removed so that all the growth sits on top of the branches in a rounded mound.*

3 *A tiered shape is ideal for* Ternstroemia gymnanthera. *It is also used for* Cryptomeria japonica, Camellia sasanqua, C. japonica, Taxus cuspidata *and* Ilex crenata.

4 *Some taller shrubs can produce a number of very attractive main stems. Clear away small twigs and weak growth from the lower parts of these stems, and trim the foliage into a rounded crown. This type of styling suits enkianthuses,* Styrax japonicus, Lindera triloba, Clethra barbinervis, Disanthus cercidifolius,

Spiraea japonica *and* Cornus officinalis, *as well as shorter trees such as* Prunus japonica, Cornus kousa, Stewartia pseudocamellia, Quercus glauca *and varieties of* Acer palmatum. *The*

Japanese red pine is also occasionally seen in this form.

5 *A pine tree can be trained to stretch a branch over a gateway. This type of topiary is suitable for the most formal areas*

around a house, usually by the front gate.

6 *Some trees, such as the Japanese yew (*Taxus cuspidata*),* Podocarpus macrophyllus *and some Japanese maples and*

oaks, produce straight, upright branches from the trunk. As with pine trees, any stems growing sideways or downwards are removed in order to create neat, rounded clusters at the ends of the branches.

left: *This 'pom-pom' style is often applied to the Japanese box (*Buxus microphylla var. japonica*) and the box-leaved holly (*Ilex crenata*), as well as to the Japanese yew (*Taxus cuspidata*).*

right: *Pine trees can be restricted in height to suit the size of a garden. This photograph shows how good pruning has encouraged all the fine branches to grow upwards, producing the characteristic bun-shaped clusters of healthy needles. These established pines no longer need to have their main branches supported with bamboo canes.*

left: *The bamboo canes and dyed black hemp rope used to train this Japanese white pine have become decorative features in their own right.*

right: Ternstroemia gymnanthera *used to be indispensable in Japanese gardens. This example, from Ritsurin Park in Takamatsu, is pruned in the traditional way with the number of side branches radically reduced to give the tree an airy look. The bamboo fence in the foreground is in the yotsume style. It is also often constructed using groups of two vertical canes instead of one.*

group of taller, more slender trees. They are often placed in the garden to suggest well-weathered, well-rounded rocks, which themselves symbolize Nature's timelessness, age and harmony.

Of all the shapes found in Japanese gardens, the most striking must be the clipped pines and yews which are made to look like giant bonsai. In the West, in the nineteenth century, opinion was divided

above: *Azaleas,* Photinia glabra, Cleyera japonica, *and various bamboo grasses are not only pruned singly but often collectively as a single wide mass. This may be any shape or width, and it can serve various purposes in the garden, acting as tall ground-cover or hedges within a garden, or even simulating rocks and hills.*

between those who dismissed them as grotesque and those who found the shapes bizarre but were at least prepared to acknowledge the skill involved in training them. Even today, in spite of changing fashions in Japan, these elaborately trained evergreens are still found in domestic gardens as well as in distinguished temple parks.

On each of a pine's severely reduced number of branches, the needles nestle like mounds of moist snow. The undersides of the branches are cleared of

needles, so that the flowing lines of the trunk and the branches are clearly visible — hence the Japanese enthusiasm for the somei-yoshino cherry, whose immense clusters of snowy pink blossoms seem to float like clouds above leafless, black, arching branches. The style of topiary which produces this effect is known in the West as "cloud pruning". Along with pines, trees suiting this style include *Ilex integra, Chamaecyparis obtusa* var. *breviramea, C. pisifera* "Plumosa", *Taxus cuspidata* and *Osmanthus heterophyllus,* as well as broadleaf evergreens such as *Quercus phillyraeoides* and *Camellia japonica.* Camellias pruned in this way look very stylish in courtyard gardens. Cloud-pruned trees are used in dry-landscape gardens and are frequently seen in Japan in front gardens. They play a major role as specimen trees in hill-and -pond gardens, but it is important that the size of the trees should be in keeping with the size of the particular garden and the distance from which they are intended to be viewed.

Should you wish to create a cloud-pruned tree from scratch, it is necessary to select a healthy sapling with a promising shape, a strong central trunk and established lateral branches. Of the latter, choose those which will provide the framework for your tree and remove the rest. The remaining branches should then be pruned back to within 60 to 90 cm (2 to 3 ft) of the trunk, the aim being to encourage new bushy growth at the tip of each of them. The best time to do this is early spring, but only after the risk of frost has passed. On some trees, the lateral branches will need to be coaxed into a more open position and secured. Leave the new growth to develop for about three years, stopping the growth at the end of the branches when they have reached their desired length. Then the foliage can be pruned into shape. Remove the side branches on the underside of the laterals to create the cloud effect.

Ilex crenata, Podocarpus macrophyllus and *Taxus cuspidata* var. *nana* are also suitable for this treatment. Because

facing page: *Another border at Ryoan-ji is planted with trees but not in order of their height. A woodland effect is produced by restricting the number of plants and meticulously refining their shapes. Shrubs such as* Euonymus japonicus *scattered among the trees help to fill empty spaces without distracting the eye.*

they are pliant, it may be preferable to use on them a technique which is used for pines, where the trunks are trained to curve in a sinuous line. It is true that in Japan this kind of topiary is an art practised by professional gardeners, but there is nothing to stop an adventurous amateur from giving it a try.

A tree will begin to take shape after about five years, but it will take as much as fifteen to twenty years for it to mature into its final form. The subject should already have reached the desired height and size before it is trained. It should have been planted in its final site for at least a year, preferably at an angle to the ground which makes shaping the trunk somewhat easier. The primary curve should be in the bottom half of the tree. Support the upper part of the curved trunk with a sturdy cane, and use another to hold this support in place. A good, sturdy branch should grow outwards from the arc formed by the trunk. This branch should be allowed to grow longer than the rest of the side branches. There should also be another, shorter side branch growing in the opposite direction lower down the trunk; this serves to counterbalance the tree's longest branch. The overall number of branches should be reduced so that the ones remaining are more or less evenly spaced along the central trunk and point in all directions around the tree. Gently bend them downwards for a more open shape, and support them with bamboo, securing these canes in turn to the trunk with rope. Prune away all the twigs on the underside of the branches. The work should be carried out between late winter and early spring, and in the case of pines it should be undertaken before the new buds begin to break.

The point of this type of Japanese topiary is to create a sense of balance through asymmetry. It involves finding a balance between the vertical pull of the trunk and the horizontal line of the branches. There are many uses for this kind of topiary in

Japanese gardens. A single specimen pine (either the Japanese black or red pine) is often grown at an angle next to the main garden gate, and trained so that one of its branches extends over it like an arch. Pines are also trained to hang over ponds and lakes, so that the reflection of their branches in the water can be enjoyed by the visitor.

It will come as no surprise that pines are meticulously pruned to preserve their elegant shape. The process has two stages. In the middle of spring, the number of new buds is reduced to two or three on each branch. Those which are either weak or too vigorous should be pinched off: in the case of *Pinus densiflora* (Japanese red pine) and *P. parviflora* (Japanese white pine), the size of the remaining buds should be reduced by a quarter to a third, while *P. thunbergii* (Japanese black pine) can have its buds reduced by a half or more. In the autumn, the tree is stripped of its old needles by rubbing each branch gently between the hands from its base towards its tip. The needles growing on the last 7 cm (3 in) or so at the end of each branch are left, for this should be the current year's growth. This procedure is particularly necessary if the buds have not been trimmed back in the spring. Less drastic grooming will be sufficient if greater growth is desired.

Arranging trees and shrubs

Topiary yews in the shape of globes, pyramids and obelisks helped to emphasize the symmetrical harmony of the gardens of the great French seventeenth-century chateaux of Vaux-le-Vicomte and Versailles. Japanese gardening, in contrast, seeks harmony in asymmetry. We have seen this in the design of topiary, and the same applies to the arrangement of trees and shrubs. Instead of working with even numbers of plants, Japanese gardeners think in odd numbers. The basic unit is composed of three trees (or tall shrubs) of differing heights, shapes

and textures, arranged in the form of a scalene triangle, that is, a triangle with sides of unequal lengths. The principal tree should be in the middle but set back at varying distances from the other two. These two latter trees (or shrubs) should be of different heights, with the shortest brought forward of the other. When arranged in this way, none of the plants will be completely hidden from view. According to traditional planting schemes for large hill-and-pond gardens, this basic group of three, when planted on a hillock, is accompanied by two even shorter shrubs to anchor the whole arrangement. These shrubs are distributed in such a way as to form more scalene triangles with relation to one or the other of the main trees. Finally, a tall tree is planted behind the hillock in order to create a feeling of distance.

The idea of the scalene triangle is used to calculate how far apart to set three plants in relation to each other, while at the same time avoiding symmetry. It is also an important tool for producing

a feeling of depth to the garden, by creating a foreground and a middle ground, with the third tree linking the two. In a garden which is wider than it is deep, the basic group of three can be balanced by positioning a group of two trees elsewhere in the garden, bringing the total to five plants.

Designing Japanese-style gardens involves discovering a pleasing balance in the asymmetry which is created when diverse types of plants are brought together. Juxtaposing deciduous trees or shrubs with evergreens ensures interest all the year round. Begin by choosing the tree that will form the central focus of the entire planting scheme. Allow its habit to suggest which trees or shrubs might go well with it. These should help to counterbalance any peculiar characteristics the principal tree might have — perhaps the way it leans in a certain direction or the general shape formed by its branches.

A classical combination is a conifer, such as a pine or an *Ilex crenata* (box-leaved holly), with a Japanese maple, adding a bushy, shorter evergreen, such as *Citrus tachibana* or *Cleyera japonica*, to give stability to the

above: *Pruned pine trees look superb against the whiteness of the gravel here in the Flat Garden at the Portland Japanese Garden.*

group. Pines and maples could also be planted beside a deciduous shrub, such as *Corylopsis pauciflora*, to let more light into the garden. A tall, fully grown camellia would also serve admirably as the focus of a group, combined, for example, with an evergreen such as *Ilex crenata* (box-leaved holly), clipped into a globe, and the softer green of a satsuki azalea. Azaleas are perhaps the most versatile plants in the Japanese garden. Not only can they be pruned singly, they can also be treated together to form a broad swathe or a low, narrow hedge to mark or separate distinct areas within the garden. Popular plants such as maples, satsuki azaleas and *Pieris japonica* (Japanese andromeda) are reliable companions for space-filling evergreens such as *Ternstroemia gymnanthera* or *Daphniphyllum macropodum*.

Hedges

Formal clipped evergreen hedges are frequently used as a background to rectilinear dry-landscape gardens. Their use helps to accentuate the geometric shape of the garden. Their height is determined by the depth of the garden and how much of the vista beyond the hedge is to be retained as part of the overall design. The borrowed vista is an important element in the composition of many ancient dry-landscape gardens found at Zen Buddhist temple gardens in Kyoto. Bearing in mind that, in Japan, smaller rectilinear gardens, which were designed principally to be viewed from the house, tended to be wider than they were deep, the straight horizontal line produced by the top of the hedge (or wall) played an important role in dividing the visual plane. The garden at the famous temple Entsu-ji cleverly manipulates perspective, by having Japanese cedars and hinoki cypresses, with their tall straight trunks carefully shorn of lower lateral branches, planted, some just inside and others outside, the evergreen hedge, beyond which, towering above the entire scene, is the distant view of Mt. Hiei, the tallest mountain in the vicinity of Kyoto.

If you wish to completely shut out the distant view, you could plant a screen of taller growing trees. Even in such cases, a dense straight hedge in front of these trees will be effective in imparting a feeling of formality to the garden, creating the illusion that there is woodland beyond the hedge.

In another rectilinear dry-landscape garden in Kyoto, this time at the temple Koho-an, there is a double row of hedges clipped to different heights to represent the surf rolling ashore. Japanese pines (a tree traditionally employed as windbreaks along sandy beaches in Japan) have been planted between the two hedges to bolster this conceit.

Hedges of various heights are used, of course, in other types of Japanese gardens as screens and boundary markers. While conifers, such as *Juniperus chinensis* "Kaizuka", *Taxus cuspidata* var. *nana* and *Podocarpus macrophyllus* var. *maki* are employed for this purpose, many of the popular plants for clipped hedges in Japan are broadleaf evergreens such as live oaks (especially *Quercus myrsinifolia*), box-leaved holly (*Ilex crenata*), *Photinia glabra* (and its more vigorous relation *Photinia x fraseri* "Red Robin"), Japanese spindle (*Euonymus japonicus*), Japanese wax-leaf privet (*Ligustrum japonicum*), sweet viburnum (*Viburnum odoratissimum*) and *Osmanthus heterophyllus*, with its holly-like leaves. *Osmanthus fragrans* f. *aurantiacus*, which has glossy leaves and intensely scented orange flowers in early autumn, forms a tight shrub when pruned and is also used for hedges, although it is not winter hardy in cooler climates. *Camellia japonica* can be grown in a row to create a tall screen. *Loropetalum chinense*, an evergreen belonging to the witch hazel family, can produce a very showy hedge. It may be left unclipped for an informal look, but it can also take pruning. Plant well-grown, bushy specimens at intervals of approximately 30cm (1ft), and stop them when they reach the desired height, so as to encourage the growth of lateral branches. There are varieties which retain a reddish tinge to their leaves all year round and others which turn green during the summer. The strap-like flowers come in a range of colours, from white to rich crimson, through to plum and purple.

Camellia sasanqua is frequently used in hedges,

possible to incorporate deciduous vines and shrubs, or even short trees such as Japanese maples. Mixed planting is also used in other kinds of topiary in Japanese gardens. Two or more species of evergreen shrubs, such as *Ligustrum japonicum* and *Photinia glabra*,

above: *One of the largest stroll gardens in Japan, found at Shugakuin Imperial Villa, was constructed in the middle of the seventeenth century.*

sometimes by itself, but more often as part of a mixed planting scheme, to which it adds bursts of colour in the autumn. Mixed planting is a way of bringing variety to a neatly clipped straight hedge. Plants used for this purpose in Japan include *Quercus phillyraeoides*, *Ligustrum japonicum* and *Photinia glabra*, along with *Camellia sasanqua* and *Osmanthus fragrans*. It is even

are sometimes grown and pruned together to create a single bush. The famous garden at the Kyoto temple Shoden-ji has a large, clipped bush consisting of satsuki azaleas, a dwarf gardenia, a live oak and *Photinia glabra*.

Low-growing shrubs of one type, such as *Taxus cuspidata* var. *nana* or satsuki azaleas, are sometimes planted together and clipped to create a thick, rounded, sinuous line running through a hill-and-pond garden. These are not so much hedges as a design motif introducing different shapes, colour and textures into the garden.

Traditional hedging plants used in Japan (please note that not all of these are frost-hardy):

Very low hedges up to 60cm (2ft): satsuki azaleas (*Rhododendron indicum* varieties), *Serrisa foetida*.

Low hedges from 90 to 120cm (3 to 4ft): *Camellia japonica, C. sasanqua, C. sinensis, Gardenia augusta "Radicans", Photinia glabra, Ilex crenata, Serrisa foetida, Ligustrum japonicum, Euonymus japonicus, Rhaphiolepis umbellata, Photinia glabra, Eurya japonica, Cleyera japonica, Taxus cuspidata* var. *nana*.

Taller hedges from 120 to 180cm (4 to 6ft): *Euonymus japonicus, Ilex integra, Quercus myrsinifolia, Q. phillyraeoides, Q. glabra, Eurya japonica, Ligustrum japonicum, Loropetalum chinensis, Camellia sasanqua, Photinia glabra, Juniperus chinensis "Kaizuka", Cleyera japonica, Corylopsis pauciflora, Elaeagnus x ebbingei, Phyllostachys bambusoides, Bambusa multiplex* var. *elegans*.

Informal hedges (minimum pruning): *Rhaphiolepis umbellata, Serrisa foetida, Camellia japonica, Podocarpus macrophylla* var. *maki, Loropetalum chinensis, Euonymus alatus, Deutzia crenata, Enkianthus perulatus*.

Mixed hedges: *Gardenia augusta "Radicans", Camellia sinensis, C. sasanqua, Euonymus alatus, Osmanthus fragrans, O. x fortunei, O. heterophyllus, Ligustrum japonicum, Euonymus japonicus, Ilex crenata, Photinia glabra, Quercus phillyraeoides*.

Choosing plants

Many attractive shrubs and grasses commonly seen in Japanese gardens have been introduced to the West, particularly since the middle of the nineteenth century. Some, unfortunately, have escaped into the wild and become invasive in their host countries, especially in warmer regions of the continental United States, as well as in Australia, New Zealand and South Africa. They include the Japanese knotweed in Britain, and the notorious kudzu vine in America. Other well-known shrubs, such as *Euonymus alatus, Ligustrum japonicum* (Japanese privet) and *Berberis thunbergii* (Japanese barberry), as well as ornamental grasses, especially of the *Miscanthus* and *Imperata* genii, have become problematical in some countries, although not so much in colder regions of Europe.

Many invasive foreign introductions are spread by seed, often carried by birds attracted to the fruit. Others spread by means of tough roots which are difficult to eradicate. Bamboos, for example, can be divided into two types: the running kind which sends out aggressive, spreading rhizomes and therefore has the potential to become very invasive; and the clump-forming kind (which includes the *Bambusa* and *Fargesia* genii), which does not produce long rhizomes and are much less likely to become invasive. Care needs to taken when planting running bamboo, especially in warmer climates: as well as using a specialist root barrier, dig a shallow trench around the bed of bamboo and cut away rhizomes as they spread into the trench.

Japanese gardens use broadleaf evergreens as the foundation of their planting schemes, mixing in conifers along with deciduous trees and flowering plants to add seasonal interest. While there are specific trees and shrubs which have become closely associated with Japanese gardens, because they hold a special place in the heart of the Japanese or have proved amenable to particularly distinctive pruning

left: *The pillar-like trunk of conifers such as the* hinoki cypress *(*Chamaecyparis obtusa*)* and the Japanese cedar *(*Cryptomeria japonica*) helps to frame the view of the distant landscape. In the foreground, the petals of a* Magnolia stellata *shrub adds brightness to the scene like a multitude of silken white ribbons.*

styles, there is, of course, no set group of plants which absolutely have to be employed.

North America possesses a wide variety of deciduous trees and shrubs producing fantastic autumn colours which would be the envy of any garden in Japan. The flowering dogwood, *Cornus florida*, is already a firm favourite in Japan. *Sassafras albidum* also produces a wonderful autumn show and is, at the same time, tolerant of pruning. Try it against a backdrop of broadleaf evergreens, or together with the eastern red cedar *Juniperus virginiana* and an abelia, or a taller evergreen azalea such as "Stewartstonian" or "Herbert", to form the basic group-of-three arrangement. The strawberry tree, *Arbutus unedo*, a native of southern Europe, and the Chilean myrtle *Luma apiculata* are just two examples of evergreens which possess superb bark and flowers, and they too can take pruning. Various different styles can be applied to them: they can be presented as a dense rounded shrub, as a multi-trunk shrub, or as a short specimen tree. There is endless scope for adapting a Japanese approach to plants which are indigenous to different environments around the world.

Rocks

The importance of rocks in Japanese gardens cannot be overstated, for the veneration of sacred rocks goes back to the earliest times. Rocks for the garden are chosen on the basis of their colour, their grain and the way they have been worn by the elements. Whether they have been scarred by volcanic activity or polished smooth by the ceaseless motion of waves, their attractiveness is thought to depend greatly on their power to evoke images and reflections. Rocks are set in Japanese gardens with the same view to the future with which trees were planted in the great English landscape gardens of the eighteenth century; the gardener looks to the future, to a time when the rocks will have been all but buried in moss.

Shapes and types of rock

There are several basic classifications of rock shapes, and each has its uses. The most important shape is that of the tall standing rock. Others include broad horizontal rocks (which may be more or less flat, uneven or step-shaped on top), very low flat rocks, round rocks, rocks in the shape of a low mound and rocks that lean diagonally. The last two are particularly useful for suggesting some of the geological changes the earth has undergone. A low, smooth, mound-like rock can make us think of the power of erosion, while a sharply slanting rock can look as though it has just been thrust up from the depths of the earth.

Since Japan is made up of a chain of igneous islands, the kind of rock most commonly found is volcanic: andesite, granite, chorite and basalt. Another much-prized type of rock seen in older gardens in

Japan is chlorite schist, which is found in a range of colours from blue- to purple-tinged greens. Rock is also classified according to its terrain – mountain, river, valley or sea coast – for rocks will have weathered in different ways depending on where they have been collected.

Choosing rocks

Just as there are stringent regulations all over the world on taking plants or animals from the wild, inanimate objects like rocks must likewise not be removed from their natural environment. They must always be obtained from an approved source. All over Japan there are now strict controls regarding river stone, for which there is still a great demand for both gardening and building. Since the Japanese have always valued naturally shaped stone over quarried stone, this poses a serious

problem if there is no standard way of acquiring the former. In some places it may be possible to obtain rock that has been cleared from land intended for new fields or buildings. Otherwise, look for local quarries and take advice from local Japanese garden societies. It is a question of making the best use of locally available material, even though it may have been intended for a different purpose – for alpine rockeries, for example, or dry-stone walls.

Try to choose rocks which do not have a square-cut appearance that makes them look like rejected building material. Avoid sharp edges and right angles; they make the rock look plain and rough at the same time. Energy and movement on the one hand, and refinement, elegance and mellowness on the other are all desirable qualities. Look for interesting contours, surfaces and colours; clearly marked strata, for example, give a sense of history and the passage of time. Tufa, a porous rock found with mineral deposits, has a unique texture and surface, but it has also been popular in the West for centuries, and supplies are diminishing. Many limestone areas are perilously close to disappearing altogether, for which reason limestone must not be used unless it is definitely known to be second-hand stone quarried a long time ago. Weathered, second-hand slate is also available sometimes.

facing page: *Japanese gardens strive for a sense of harmony with Nature by trying to integrate the man-made with what is natural. In this garden by Terry Welch, the wooden planks used for the gate blend beautifully with the landscape of native conifers, while the contrast between the natural grace of the firs and the refined beauty of the pruned pines draws attention to the powers and limitations of human creativity.*

Herbaceous plants, such as tall Japanese anemones (perhaps the white single "Honorine Jobert", "Géant des Blanches", or the pink "Max Vogel") can be used in a garden of this type.

Arranging rocks

It is important that rocks should be laid so they look as if they belong naturally in the landscape. For example, they are much more interesting when they give the illusion of being the tip of something vast lying hidden underground. Thus they are often set so that the rock seems to emerge from the ground at its broadest part. A rock that swells gently out of the ground reproduces the archetypal, maternal shape of Japanese mountains. Rocks that look precarious are frowned upon. They should never be set in such a way that they taper towards ground level.

If a particular rock has blemishes, sharp corners or a bad shape, it may be possible to disguise its imperfections by using it in combination with other rocks or with low, ground-hugging shrubs. However, rocks will always have more of an impact if there are not too many of them cluttering an area. Go for fewer, larger rocks rather than an array of smaller pieces. An alternative is to work out an arrangement in which only the

attractive parts of the rocks emerge above ground level. A single rock can be incorporated into the top of a man-made mound so that the only visible part of its surface, peering out of the moss, can seems like the bare face of a miniature mountain. It is also important to remember that newly planted shrubs and trees will eventually grow and make those precious rocks look smaller than they did when everything was first laid out. Although a newly planted garden will inevitably look bare, it is important to try to anticipate how the mature plants will eventually balance the groups of rocks and any other inanimate features you might wish to include, such as stone lanterns and fences.

Often a single, imposing rock gives an austere dignity to a garden, particularly at the front of a house. It can stand alone in gravel, or it can be embellished with low shrubs, a small tree such as a Japanese maple, or a perennial with interesting foliage, for instance, *Farfugium japonicum*. On the other hand, it can be surrounded by elegant tall canes of bamboo which have

Arranging groups of stones

1 *The base of a rock should always be set in the ground so that the visible part of it looks broader nearer the gound (a). It should never taper towards the ground (b).*

2 *The basic group of three rocks should be arranged so that they form a scalene triangle when seen from the side.*

3 *The shape of the biggest and central stone of any group determines the feel of the landscape they create. A tall, rough, upright*

stone suggests a craggy mountain landscape, while a smooth, low stone resembles an ancient, eroded hill in miniature.

4 *A group of three rocks should be laid out so that their highest points form a rough scalene triangle when seen from above. The idea of the scalene triangle is not a fixed rule, but a useful tool to use when considering how far apart and in what sort of relation to each other the stones should be arranged.*

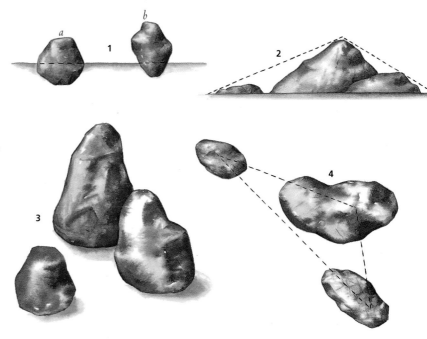

been carefully stripped of their lower branches. A rock of this kind, as well as tilted stones, must be carefully set and braced underground with more stones, so that they are absolutely secure and cannot topple over.

Combinations of more than two rocks should be of the same material, even if their size and shape are different. The idea is that they should look as if they all belong together. The basic unit is once again the group of three, in the shape of a scalene triangle. Show off the main rock of the group to its best advantage. Like human faces, rocks have their best side, although some ruggedness may be attractive in either. The oldest advice on arranging stones comes to us from the eleventh century: give a rock what it cries out for. Give it what it needs to make it look secure and stable. Any additional stones are there to complement the principal piece. Japanese gardens have always sought to create a sense of balance and harmony out of what appears to be asymmetrical. Avoid setting out the rocks in a row or at right angles to each other. The whole group should look stable and solid together; the rocks should not look as though they are precariously propping each other up. Around the main group of three, an arrangement can be expanded to include ultimately five, seven or even fifteen stones.

The principal rock should be set so that its face is turned slightly sideways when seen from the front. Another point to keep in mind is that in a stroll garden a group of rocks should be interesting when seen from different angles. One trick to give added depth to your garden is to place larger rocks in the foreground and smaller ones in the distance, so they look further away than they really are. The same strategy can be applied to the placing of trees, where delicately branched trees are deliberately planted in the distance. A solid stone which seems to reach up to the sky imparts a sense of calm dignity and adds gravitas to a garden. Many rocks, on the other hand, leaning towards one side or

another, draw the eye in a particular direction. Groups of rocks can exploit this to help create the dynamics of the garden, and their shapes can determine the principal direction in which the eye of the viewer is led through the composition of the garden.

Native religious associations, with which rocks were always imbued in Japan, were reinforced by various Chinese religious traditions which, along with Buddhism, began to cross over to Japan in the fourth, fifth and sixth centuries. Buddhist mythology included several holy mountains, while the Chinese possessed their own myth of a Mountain Isle of Eternal Youth (Mount Horai in Japanese) which was thought to be inhabited by immortal wise men. By the eleventh century, groups of garden stones were being arranged to represent such sacred places.

Buddhist mountains

There are two important mountains in the Buddhist tradition in Japan. One is Mount Fudaraku, considered to be the home of Kannon, the bodhisattva of mercy. A single massive rock often has the double function of conveying an image of this fabled mountain to the initiate, while at the same time tapping more indigenous religious sentiments. The other mountain belonging to Buddhist lore is Shumisen, the mountain at the centre of the universe. Surrounded by seven seas, encircled in turn by seven golden mountains, an ocean, and finally a ring of iron mountains, Shumisen inspired cluster formations of rocks.

The Buddhist tradition of portraying various Buddhas flanked by a pair of their attendant bodhisattvas gives an added religious dimension to the basic group of three rocks. These arrangements are called *sanzonseki*, which can be translated as "stones suggesting three Buddhas". The old gardening masters, however, were superstitious about placing a three-Buddha stone group in the centre of the main view from the house. Not only did it suggest to them the imminence of

death, but it offended their sense of the rightness of asymmetry. For this reason, important features in the garden were invariably placed slightly to the left or slightly to the right of the central line of vision.

Occasionally a low flat stone is place in front of the three-Buddha grouping, not necessary close to it, but perhaps across a pond or indeed the entire garden, so that it looks towards the three-Buddha stones. This is the *reihaiseki*, or the "worship stone", representing the spot from which to venerate Buddha.

Often in dry-landscape gardens, the three-Buddha arrangement simultaneously symbolises a cascade of water flowing between boulders, or a cataract flanked on either side by cliff faces. This kind of dry-waterfall arrangement is also employed in pond gardens in lieu of a waterfall with running water.

Zen temple gardens sometimes include a big flat-topped rock on which a monk might practise *zazen*, or meditation. More unusual is the boat-shaped rock, which can be seen in pond gardens, as well as in dry-landscape gardens where the water is symbolised by gravel. This represents a celestial boat which, according to Japanese mythology, descended to earth from the skies in the time of the gods. There is also a Chinese tradition of a heavenly boat which conveys the seven gods of good fortune. Sometimes a boat-shaped stone is found in conjunction with a stone symbolising Mount Horai, the Island of Eternal Youth.

Representations of Mount Horai can be distinguished from Buddhist mountains because they often

above: *Large garden stones in Japanese gardens are not always intended to be symbolic. Often they are chosen for their beauty and character to serve as a focal point, as here in this garden, which has been created at the foot of a steep slope that has been incorporated into the garden's overall design.*

double as an image of one of two sacred creatures: turtles, which were thought to support Mount Horai on their backs, and cranes, on which the immortal sages were supposed to ride. Turtle rocks are quite common and are easily identified, though the turtle is usually represented only by one or another of its body parts – most often its outstretched neck and head, occasionally its legs, tail and shell. Sometimes the turtle is represented by a small island, with a rock in its centre representing Mount Horai, and a pine, the tree sacred to Chinese sages, planted nearby. Cranes are usually represented by a stubby triangular stone signifying an outstretched wing. Occasionally stones are chosen to represent their long necks or their tails. Both turtle and crane rocks can be found in pond gardens and surrounded by sand in dry-landscape gardens.

Placing rocks

Garden stones help to impart an ageless quality to gardens. Their placement is crucial in determining the layout of the landscape in all types of Japanese gardens. When creating a garden, the first thing a Japanese considers is where the principal rock – the largest, most imposing, and beautiful one – should be placed. This is usually the most important decision, for everything else follows on from it. At Chion-in Temple, Kyoto, the smaller of the two gardens facing the hall holds twenty-six stones set among an undulating sea of clipped azaleas. One rock dominates the entire garden: this represents Buddha. When the azaleas are in bloom, it looks as though Buddha is descending in glory on shimmering clouds, accompanied by a host of bodhisattvas. The composition is borrowed from a painting preserved at Chion-in Temple. At Jizo-in Temple, also in Kyoto, sixteen stones represent monks who have attained serene enlightenment.

left: *The similarity of shape between the rocks and the pruned shrubs serves to highlight the differences between the inanimate and the living. This is an important though unobtrusive theme in many dry-landscape gardens. The stone grouping here represents a turtle, an auspicious symbol of longevity. The round stone at the far end symbolises its head.*

Water

If rocks symbolize Japan's mountainous terrain, water in the garden represents the swift rivers and tranquil lakes of the country, and the broad seas by which she is surrounded. Islands in the middle of ponds and lakes, sometimes nothing more than a few outcrops of rock, reflect the country's self-image as an archipelago scattered across the open sea.

Ponds

Ponds tend to be irregular in shape, as the aim is to create a naturalistic look. However, there are certain shapes which caught the fanciful imagination of early gardening masters, and allowed them to add another layer of symbolism to their designs. One is the cloud shape, another is the bottle gourd. Then there are a couple of traditional shapes based on the calligraphic rendering of Chinese pictograms: one is the word for water, the other the word for spirit or soul. All of these flowing shapes produce an interestingly varied shoreline, and for this reason ponds and lakes have continued to be designed with them in mind.

The edges of a pond can be adorned with aquatic or marginal plants. The most popular by far are Japanese water irises: *Iris laevigata* and *I. ensata*. The latter needs to be kept out of water after it has finished flowering and over the winter. Plant irises in swathes for their handsome leaves and their purple, mauve, lavender or white blossoms. *Iris pseudacorus* (the yellow flag iris of Europe) and *Iris versicolor* (the blue flag iris of North America) are good alternatives. *Acorus calamus* (sweet flag or sweet rush), with its aromatic, slender leaves, is also very attractive; so is its

Japanese relation, *Acorus gramineus*. Further away from the shore, water-lilies can be grown in clumps so that their leaves eventually form green circles that contrast with the open water.

Do not allow aquatic plants to cover the entire pond. The pleasure of an open expanse of water is often enhanced by keeping the planting to a minimum and letting the water act as a mirror to the clouds, lanterns, rocks and waterside trees. In warmer climates *Nelumbo nucifera* (sacred lotus), perhaps the most perfect aquatic flower of all, can be grown in large garden ponds or lakes. Symbolic of the human soul in Buddhism, they have a unique elegance, holding their perfectly shaped, pointed buds high above their leaves; when the petals unfold, each one looks as though it has been cut from the most delicate silk. The flowers also have a marvellous scent.

right: *A yatsuhashi* (zig-zag) *bridge makes an ideal path through shallow water planted with aquatic and marginal plants. This low type of bridge helps to create the feeling that one is walking among the plants. It makes it possible to see up close the frilly delicacy and exquisite markings of* Iris ensata. *This example is from the Japanese Garden in Portland, Oregon.*

facing page: *Hill-and-pond stroll gardens can be designed to fit a surprising range of sizes. This is a very intimate example from the United States. Instead of a wooden ornamental bridge, a simple footbridge has been put together using stone slabs. Lanterns with curved legs are used exclusively over water.*

Perennials such as astilbe and filipendula, with their open sprays of flowers, and foliage plants, such as Astilboides tabularis *and* Rodgersia podophylla, *would suit the wet margins of informal ponds such as this one.*

Creating sand-bars or a pebble or shingle beach is one of the oldest traditions in Japanese gardening. These can be made to resemble anything from a desolate seashore to the appealing bank of a pleasantly cool mountain lake. Sometimes a long headland of pebbles is created across a narrow section of a

other hand, create the feeling of wild, wave-swept sea cliffs. In these settings rocks should be used with discretion; too many will reduce the overall impact. It is important always to place them where they look as though they belong. When selecting rocks for water features, try to find pieces which suggest the activity

pond, clearly referring to one of the most famous traditional sights along the Sea of Japan, a long sand spit known as Ama-no-hashidate or the Bridge to Heaven.

Large rocks are often arranged around the edge of ponds, particularly where a smooth bank of *Zoysia japonica* (Japanese carpet grass) descends right down to the water. These banks produce a mellow pastoral effect, especially if the pond is given a gently curving shoreline. Craggier rocks and a jagged shore, on the

of water; for example, one convention involves placing a large, flattish boulder along the outer shore of a bend in a stream. The rock then looks as if it is actually directing the course of the water, and becomes an integral part of the design of the stream.

All of these ways of embellishing a bank allow the gardener to create his or her own image of Nature while protecting the edge from erosion. Still, there are alternatives to a naturalistic approach. Low pine

stakes, about 10 cm (4 in) in diameter, are often
used along the edge of a pond or lake to give the
shoreline definition. They do not need to be all the
same height; instead they can be arranged so that their
tops form a wavy line. Willow or split bamboo strips
can be used to weave the poles together. A line of low
poles of this kind is also used to distinguish areas
where water irises are planted, so that they do not
look too straggly.

Waterfalls

Waterfalls and cascades marry together the image of
mountain heights with the attraction of flowing
water. They can be thin or broad, overhanging or
meandering, or broken by rocks. They may consist of
two or three steps.

A basic arrangement of four rocks is traditionally
used for waterfalls. The largest serves as the backdrop
for the falling water, and it is supported by one
boulder on each side . These can be flanked in turn by
smaller rocks. At the base of the falls, a smoother
rock protrudes slightly above the surface of the water;
this indicates where the water hits the pool and helps
to part the stream. Sometimes a rock for this spot was
chosen to represent a carp, after a Chinese legend
about a carp that climbed a waterfall and became a
dragon that then rose up to Heaven. An extra couple
of rocks can be placed further downstream to
emphasize the direction of the current. If a long, flat
rock is being used as a bridge, it too should be placed
slightly downstream so as not to block the view of the
waterfall. Stepping-stones across the stream make an
attractive alternative. This type of arrangement can be
used in dry-landscape gardens as well, for it is very
effective with sand or fine gravel representing a
flowing stream.

Ground-hugging vegetation is usually planted
around the source of the water above the falls. To
conceal it further, an evergreen is placed at the top of

the falling water. A Japanese maple, a pine or a weeping willow is usually planted next to the waterfall so that its branches partly conceal it. The sight of cascading water glimpsed through a veil of delicate foliage is often considered a finer thing than a completely exposed view, for it adds a sense of mystery and depth to the whole composition.

Creating water features

Designing a water feature is an integral part of deciding on an overall landscape for the garden. It might be a mountain pool surrounded by tall rocks and evergreen shrubs, or a lake in grassy open countryside. A waterfall, a spring-fed basin, a rippling brook or a lazy, winding stream — all are possibilities.

In a domestic garden, a water feature can be created by using convenient pre-formed ponds, which are readily available from garden suppliers. Some people may wish to design their own ponds, incorporating various planting schemes and groups of rocks. In these cases, the generally recommended way of securing the sides and the bottom of the pond is to use concrete over a bed of hardcore. When digging out the pond, it is important to allow for the combined thickness of the layers of hardcore and concrete. Check that the pond is level, using a plank and a spirit level. The layer of hardcore should be up to 15 cm (6 in) thick and firmly compacted. The concrete (1 part cement to 3 parts sand to 6 parts grit) goes on top of this and should be 10 cm (4 in) thick. Put in wire reinforcing mesh to strengthen the walls and bottom of the pond.

It is a good idea to have the walls of the pond sloping outwards, for this will ensure that the concrete will not crack if ice forms on the surface of the water. If the sides slope, it will probably also be possible to apply the concrete without using a frame. If the walls are perpendicular, however, a frame made of plywood boards will be necessary as a mould into

Setting a rock at the edge of a pool

right: *If the pond is large, it is often easier to incorporate the ledge when first digging it out. Sloping, shallow edges will make it unnecessary to build a frame into which to pour the concrete. It is important to make sure that there are no cracks in the concrete or the mortar, particularly around the rocks.*

any space left between the rock and the bank is filled with soil and planted with ground-cover

cement

mortar should be used to smooth the join between rock and shelf

hardcore

Traditional pond shapes

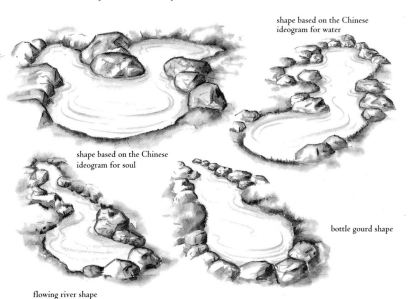

shape based on the Chinese ideogram for water

shape based on the Chinese ideogram for soul

bottle gourd shape

flowing river shape

facing page: *A pool fed by a cascade is an ideal spot for a sheltered bench. A wisteria pergola could be constructed instead, for it will have a cool canopy of light green leaves during the summer and earlier in the year it will be hung with clusters of blossom. Shades of purple look particularly striking when seen against a backdrop of green. They are very beautiful near water if used with restraint as they are here in the Honda Tea Garden designed by J. Dowle and K. Ninomiya for the Chelsea Flower Show in 1995 (the same garden is pictured on page 4). Various paths allow the garden to be seen from different perspectives.*

cloud shape

which to pour the concrete. Be sure to include an overflow in the design of the pond so that water will not spill out when there is heavy rain.

Underwater rocks can be secured to the bottom and sides of the pond on a bed of mortar (1 part cement to 4 parts sand). The layer of mortar should be up to 5 cm (2 in) thick. It is a good idea to paint some waterproofing agent onto the concrete before the mortar goes on (an alternative is to mix a water-proofing agent in with the concrete itself). Make sure when applying the mortar around the rocks that there are no cracks left through which the water can seep away. If there are any gaps above the water level between the rocks and the concrete, fill them in with earth. When the construction is finished, apply a sealant to the surface of the mortar to keep harmful lime from leaching into the water. Setting up groups of rocks at the edge of the water might be easier in a deep pond if there is a shelf along its rim so that the rocks can be placed in shallower water. A shelf of this kind also comes in handy for positioning aquatic plants. The pond can be dug out with various levels already incorporated, or the shelf can be built after-wards using breeze blocks. Rocks in the middle of the pond can be fixed to the bottom with mortar. A larger island for planting azaleas or even a pine can be left in place when the pond is first being dug. Remember that its sides must be waterproofed in the same way as the rest of the pond.

If the pond is intended for fish, round off any sharp edges underwater using mortar so that the fish will not injure themselves against either the sides of the pond or the rocks. Avoid releasing fish into a freshly made pond as the chemical agents in the concrete might kill them off. Leave the water to rest for a few days after construction before putting in any plants as well. Fish should not be introduced until two or more weeks after the plants.

For an average garden, the pool should not be more than 50 to 60 cm (20 to 24 in) deep, although if it is intended for big koi carp it will have to be deeper than the length of the full-grown fish. On the other hand, it can be as shallow as 30 cm (12 in). Where the bottom of the pool is visible, embed pebbles in the mortar for a more natural look. A simple way of adding aquatic and marginal plants to a pond is to use purpose-made containers, which are made of lattice-work to allow water to circulate. Con-tainers with a coarse mesh should be lined with hessian or close-woven polypropylene sheets so that soil is not washed out. These containers can rest on the bottom of the pool or, if the plants are marginals, on a shelf around the edge of the pond. As some aquatic plants require ever-deeper water as they begin to grow from spring onwards, it is easier to adjust their depth if they sit on blocks, which can be removed as necessary. Use specialist aquatic compost or garden soil enriched with bonemeal, and top-dress with gravel.

Creating a stream

When designing a stream, try to visualize the direction in which the current is flowing. A shallow, pebbly brook, for example, might develop eventually into a broad, gentle stream. A more mountainous one might have its beginnings in a waterfall or a series of small cascades. Rocks placed in the middle of a current need to look as though they belong there, and pebbly shoals should seem as though they were naturally created by the flowing water. Rocks which are carefully positioned in this way can help to emphasize the feeling of moving water.

A stream should be between 30 and 40 cm (12 to 16 in) deep, with waterside plants and rocks to evoke the idea of a natural running current. Alterna-tively, it could be very shallow, with water barely 5 cm (2 in) deep. If the bottom is then covered with gravel about 2 cm (1 in) in diameter, the water

above: *Here the designer Richard Coward juxtaposes the straight lines of the decking in the foreground with the curved shoreline created at the other end of the garden by the plants, such as the clump of* Iris laevigata.

Laying a stream bed

shrub

hardcore

concrete

stone parting the current

mortar

will produce a pleasant, soothing murmur.

Streams are constructed in the same way as ponds. If it is to be a shallow stream with slow-flowing water, the concrete can be poured after the rocks have already been set in place. Use gravel or pebbles for the bottom of the stream, embedding about a third of the material into the mortar. The remainder can be used to conceal any mortar still visible. This will ensure that the entire stream bed will not shift around in the flowing water.

It is important that there should be something in the garden suggesting the head, or source, of the stream. Garden stones can be arranged to suggest a dry waterfall or cascade. Should you want flowing water, shrubs can be used to disguise the header pool at the top of a waterfall where the water is piped in. Or the water can be made to run out from between rocks to suggest a mountain spring. Another method is to have water trickling from a bamboo spout into a stone basin which then overflows into a little rill. This arrangement is likewise meant to suggest a naturally flowing spring, and it should be designed and planted with this in mind. The actual amount of water from the bamboo spout will not be sufficient to create a current, so supplement your stream with water from another concealed source.

By giving your stream curves and bends, it will be

possible to experiment with perspective in order to give depth to your garden. By having the water level between 10 and 20 cm (4 to 8 in) lower than ground level, the brook itself will look deeper. The eye will be drawn to strategically placed rocks along its bank, or to dotted specimen trees – Japanese maples, for instance, or birches in a larger garden. The feeling of open space can be produced by planting ground-hugging plants like *Ophiopogon* or moss, or by putting stepping-stones across the stream. A solitary weeping Japanese maple can veil a bend in a winding stream in a way that adds mystery to the garden. Its impact is diminished, however, if it has to fight for attention with other plants. A tree leaning over a pool or shrubs that barely trail their leaves over the water helps to soften the lines of the stream or pond. It is not nearly as effective to overcrowd the banks with many different plants.

It is important to keep in mind where the vantage points in your garden are going to be. Make sure that your stream is not entirely obscured either by the terrain (from the stream lying too low below ground

above: *Where the bed of a stream is visible, it is important to make it decorative by putting in a layer of pebbles. A third should be embedded in the mortar so they cannot shift around in the flowing water. The rest should completely cover any exposed areas of mortar. A cascade can be incorporated into a stream by adapting the basic design used for constructing waterfalls. The rock over which the water flows is flanked on either side by slightly taller stones, each of which has in turn a shorter, chunkier stone at its base. A leaf-shaped stone is placed slightly downstream of a waterfall or cascade to divide the current. It should rise out of the water in the direction of the falling water and taper at the other end.*

A shrub, such as Callicarpa dichotoma – or a maple, willow, or pine in the case of a waterfall – can be planted by the falling water so that its branches partly veil it, softening the contours of the rocks.

level) or by the planting. If it is a small garden, the primary vantage point is inevitably going to be from the house. A stream that flows near the house will be much more interesting than one that remains in the far distance. A stream 30 to 60 cm (1 to 2 ft) wide is said to look its best from a distance of about 3 to 6 m (10 to 20 ft) away. In a larger garden, the stream can be as much as 1 to 1.5 m (3 ft 4 in to 5 ft) in width. If there is a path leading down to views of the garden, plan it so that the scenery steadily changes. Surprise your visitors. A partly concealed feature will excite their curiosity, and a turn in the path can suddenly open up an unexpected view.

To have water circulating in the garden, it will be necessary to create a pool at the bottom of the watercourse, in which a submersible pump can be installed. Water can then be pumped back up to the top of the watercourse through a flexible pipe buried under the soil (and protected by a row of narrow tiles placed on top of it so that it cannot be accidentally punctured by a probing spade). If the top end of the pipe is to be submerged in the header pool, the pipe will need to be fitted with a non-return valve so that water cannot flow the wrong way. A header pool at the top of the watercourse will also help to reserve water and minimize its loss when the pump is turned off. A series of cascades with each step slightly inclining towards the back will create little pools which will also retain water.

If you are going to have miniature cascades, the gradient of the stream bed should be between eight and ten per cent; if the stream is to be a slow flowing one, the gradient can be between one and two per cent. The longer the stream is, the higher the source of water will need to be elevated in order to create a current. Since a stone basin is usually placed on low ground, it could look out of place if, as the source of a watercourse, it is perched on top of a mound, unless a method is devised to deceive the eye so that

the ground does not seem as high as it actually is. Use a low basin and make the ground slope as gently as possible. Otherwise, plants can be used to minimize the impression of height.

When planning any kind of water feature, it is absolutely necessary to keep in mind the safety of children who might be visiting your garden. It is

important to remember that traditional Japanese-style gardens are not designed to be safe play-areas for children.

Decking is a good way of creating a low verandah that overlooks a water garden. Pruned shrubs may be used in front of low verandahs so that the drop to the level of the garden will not seem so abrupt.

facing page: *A series of shallow cascades produces a delightfully cool feeling in hot climates. Japan is exceedingly hot and humid in summer and people yearn for the sight and sound of cool mountain streams.*

above: *Water rushing among a cluster of rocks broadens into a gentle, smooth-flowing stream with a broad, pebbly shoreline which makes it look wider than it really is.*

above: *Water rushes from a bamboo spout into a stone basin and overflows into a pond. The basin is natural rock and looks as though it has been carved by the flow of water. This design expresses vividly the idea of a mountain spring.*

Stone basins

For intimate gardens too small for a pond, a water feature that incorporates a basin may be an attractive alternative. Stone basins are a particularly important feature of tea gardens and were originally intended for washing the hands and rinsing the mouth. Even if they are primarily meant to be decorative, they should still look practical and be provided with a *hishaku*, a bamboo scoop used for pouring water over the hands. Basins can be hollowed-out natural stone or elaborately sculpted in any number of traditional styles. Popular shapes include the Japanese apricot (*ume*), easily identifiable by its five rounded petals, and the multi-petalled chrysanthemum. Another familiar type is the *natsume*, a tall but squat cylindrical basin, named after the fruit of the jujube tree (*Ziziphus jujuba*) which it is said to resemble. Circular coin shapes are also common, some with Chinese characters in bas relief around the mouth: one type is called *fusen* after the Chinese coin on which it is modelled. Another, named after the Ryoan-ji Temple where its famous prototype is found, has four Chinese characters around a square mouth, the message reading "The only important thing is to know to be content". Square basins include the *ginkakuji* style, which has lattice patterns on three of its sides. Other square basins have Buddhas carved in bas relief instead, referring back to a time when old pieces of temple masonry were rescued and reused as water basins in tea gardens.

Setting up stone basins involves traditional arrangements of rocks called *tsukubai*. The basin is set low and placed next to a sump to catch overflowing water. This sump is sometimes called the "ocean". It may have pebbles embedded in its mortar lining and a few free stones concealing the drainage hole. Sometimes four or five rough stones are piled up above the hole instead, but they need to be placed so that water does not splash the user. The larger the

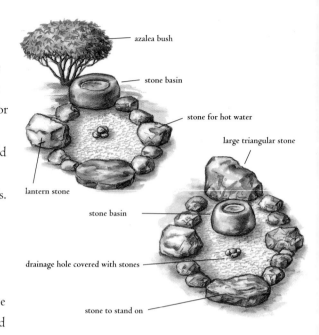

azalea bush

stone basin

stone for hot water

large triangular stone

stone basin

lantern stone

drainage hole covered with stones

stone to stand on

Stone basin arrangements

basin the shallower and wider the sump needs to be. A small basin can be placed on a short stand inside a deeper sump; however, the sump must not be deeper than any sewage system it might be connected to, so that drainage is not impeded.

Opposite the basin and across the sump, a flat, low stone provides a place stable and broad enough for an adult to stand on comfortably. This stone is generally placed at a distance of about 70 cm (2 ft 4 in) from the middle of the basin, and is larger and slightly higher than the other stepping-stones in the garden. To the right of this stone, traditional *tsukubai* will have a slightly taller flat stone where, in cold weather, a basin of hot water was placed for the use of guests attending the tea ceremony. On the left is a flat stone, again taller than the stone for the hot-water basin, where a lantern would be left for evening ceremonies. The positions of these last two stones are reversed in other traditions of the tea ceremony. A large, tall stone or an evergreen shrub is sometimes placed behind the basin to give height to the overall arrangement and to provide a sense of protection.

Sand

right: *Here at the Bloedel Reserve, Bainbridge Island, Washington, a flat, abstract, dry-landscape garden is successfully integrated with an open land-scaped garden. There is no feeling that a fence is necessary to create a special "Japanese" area. The abstract arrangement of the rocks contains three distinct groups. The one in the foreground illustrates the basic scalene triangle layout of three rocks.*

Along with running water, the simplicity of white sand evokes a sense of calm and purity in the garden. White sand has always been used in the gardens of both Shinto shrines and Buddhist temples to mark off a sacred ritual space. Sand is thus a way of bringing a spiritual dimension into the garden without reference to any specific religion. It has a significant part to play in many types of Japanese gardens. Where there may not be enough space for a water feature, sand can represent a river, a lake or even an ocean, with the added boon of eliminating the need to worry about waterproofing. More importantly, white sand can create a sense of open space in the smallest and darkest courtyard garden.

In the ancient gardens of Kyoto, the sand used was not sea sand but fine, white, decomposed granite gravel. For a sand garden, choose coarse sand or gravel with grains between 3 and 8 mm (⅛ to ⅜ in) in diameter. Obviously, sand that is too fine will blow around in the wind. Another reason for avoiding sea sand is that its smooth, round grains will not stay in place when it is raked into a pattern. An important thing to check when buying sand or gravel is its colour, both when it is dry and when it is wet.

The first step in creating a sand feature is to make the ground smooth and level. Firm the soil by rolling it well and then put in a layer of coarse gravel. On top of this goes a layer of concrete or mortar to a depth of about 5 cm (2 in). This will help to keep the sand clean and unmuddied and prevents the growth of weeds. It is important that the concrete should be provided with drainage points for

rainwater to escape, either by seeping into the gravel layer or by draining away through a pipe. Another possibility, if the area is a small one, is to use a poly-propylene sheet with holes punched into it at regular intervals. If the sand gets dirty, it can easily be hosed down. For edging the sand garden a variety of materials is used, including brick, stone, paving tiles and wood, but try to avoid plastic. The sand is laid to a depth of between 3 and 10 cm (1 ¼ and 4 in), depending on whether or not patterns are to be raked in it. The underlying concrete or polypropylene sheet must not be exposed by the patterns, which should be at least 5 cm (2 in) in depth to look effective, though they can be deeper.

Before the pattern is raked in, the sand is swept, preferably with a besom, and levelled with an implement consisting of a board attached to a long handle. Common garden rakes are now generally used for making the patterns, but many famous temples

concentric ripples

whirlpool

ocean wave

Traditional sand patterns

sideways concentric ripples

open river wave

surf pattern

stream current

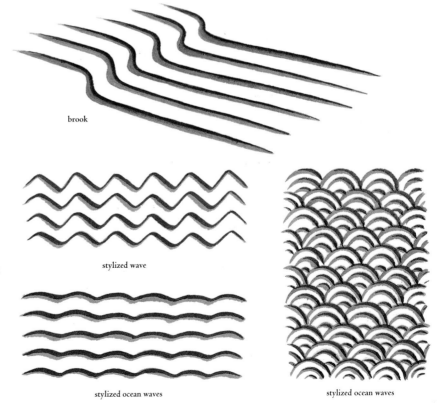

brook

stylized wave

stylized ocean waves

stylized ocean waves

have their own specially designed wooden or bamboo rakes. There are quite a number of traditional sand patterns to choose from, and there is nothing to stop the gardener from experimenting with an original design. Traditional motifs are often based on the theme of waves. Sand is used like this in dry-landscape gardens to symbolize the perpetual motion of water. Parallel, gently undulating lines can suggest a calm brook, river or ocean, depending on the width of the lines. Some designs are naturalistic, others highly stylized. There is one popular pattern representing high ocean waves which is often mistaken in the West for fish scales; it is also found as a design on fabric or paper. Whorls and spirals signify whirlpools. By raking concentric circles around a rock, it can be made to look like either a miniature outcrop of land in the middle of a minute ocean or, at the same time, a pebble or even a leaf which has just fallen into a pool of water.

Paths and stepping-stones

right: *This stone bench harmonizes well with the landscape around it.* Begonia grandis *subsp.* evansiana *is good around stone benches and water basins. Alternatives might include a drift of* Ardisia crenata, *which is particularly good with moss and has the bonus of bright red winter berries, or a* tachibana *orange shrub (*Citrus tachibana*), with its large, shiny, bright green, oval leaves.*

Stepping-stones were first used in tea gardens to provide paths while preserving the naturalistic ambience of the planting. When set in moss or among low, ground-hugging plants, stepping-stones succeed in blurring the boundaries between the planting and the path. Rather than banishing humans to footpaths, it draws people into the garden. Even when stepping-stones are meant primarily to be decorative, like stone basins they should always appear functional. Japanese gardens have evolved various stylized forms over the centuries, but each feature originally had a practical purpose which even now should not be forgotten. There is beauty in a tool which fulfils its purpose. Stepping-stones set too close next to a hedge or those which lead nowhere at all are unseemly, even if they are only meant to be ornamental. So are stones which are too far apart, awkwardly placed, or too rounded at the top.

Stepping-stones should be flat and at least 20 to 30 cm (8 to 12 in) in diameter to make walking easy and safe. Try to avoid stones which are indented towards the centre as they will collect water. They should be at least 10 cm (4 in) in thickness, and should rise between 3 and 9 cm (1 ¼ to 3 ½ in) above ground level (lower for tea gardens, higher for domestic gardens). The art of laying out stepping-stones made of natural rock lies in the skill of juxtaposing their irregular shapes against each other in such a way that they also look pleasing.

The stones are generally placed 10 cm (4 in) apart, but this depends on the size of the stones.

Calculate how far apart to set your stones, based on the length of your stride. In Japan, 50 cm (1 ft 8 in) is the usual distance allowed between the centre of one stepping-stone and the next. In tea gardens, however, a pace is considered to be slightly shorter. Anything farther apart makes walking in Japanese dress difficult. Contrary to popular notions in the West, kimonos are not loose-flowing garments. They are very tightly secured around the midriff, not with a flimsy sash, but a thick and solid length of silk. Women are expected to walk decorously without letting the skirts of their kimonos fly open. The use of traditional slippers – the thongs of which pass between the big toe and the adjoining toe – means that women tend to walk pigeon-toed as well, although men are allowed to stride a little more. All of this has implications for the way traditional

zig-zag patterns for stepping-stones have evolved.

If you have stones of different sizes, one idea is to alternate the large stones with smaller ones, keeping the distance between the centres of adjacent stones the same all the way along. Sometimes small ornamental stones are included in the design of the path. Oval stones are not only set lengthwise in the direction of the path, as might be expected, but often also horizontally to avoid overemphasizing the forward movement of the path. Another thing to avoid is having right angles where paths intersect. A stone slightly bigger than the rest can be placed on the spot where paths diverge; this will also provide an attractive vantage point in the garden. A prized specimen tree or a stone lantern is often placed near such a spot. Larger, more imposing stones are also

above: *Rocks and foliage plants are used almost exclusively here to experiment with different heights and textures. The clump of spiky irises in the foreground will provide a spot of bright colour in the garden in spring.*

left: *Stones of different sizes and shapes have been meticulously fitted together to form this imposing path leading from the front gate to the entrance of Ryugen-in Temple, belonging to the Daitoku-ji Temple complex in Kyoto.*

Symmetry has been carefully avoided in the design of this garden. A solitary boulder to the left deceives the visitor into feeling that the garden is deeper than it really is. The doorway is partly hidden behind the trees.

Though the planting is almost entirely restricted to evergreens, Osmanthus fragrans f. aurantiacus *in this kind of situation will give a heady scent in the autumn.*

The Elements of a Japanese Garden
paths and stepping-stones
111

Patterns for stepping-stones

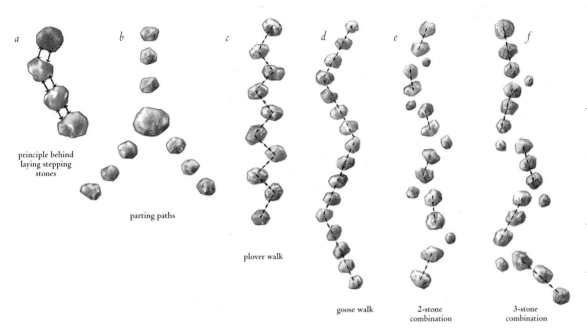

principle behind
laying stepping
stones

parting paths

plover walk

goose walk

2-stone
combination

3-stone
combination

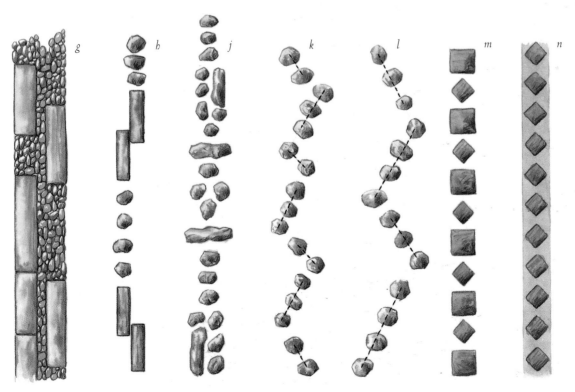

slab-and-stone
combination I

slab-and-stone
combination II

7–5–3 stone
combination

2–3 stone
combination

3–4 stone
combination

scale pattern I

scale pattern II

left: *Stepping-stones should be placed so that straight edges face each other and are roughly parallel (a). This is done so that the path looks the same width along its whole length. If two angular edges of adjacent stones face each other, the path will look as though it narrows at that point. Unless a stone is perfectly circular, it will have edges which are more or less straight.*

Where a path divides, a large flat stone, occasionally of a different type such as a mill-stone, is used as a decorative feature (b). This stone should be large enough for a person to stand on comfortably.

The plover (c) and goose (d) patterns are the basic zig-zag patterns used for stepping-stone paths. The 2–3 stone and 3–4 stone combination patterns (k and l) are adaptations of these. The 2-stone and 3-stone combinations (e and f) are designed to make the patterns as inconspicuous as possible. These are particularly good for tea gardens, where the path meanders among trees and shrubs.

The slab-and-stone combination I (g) can be used for formal paths leading up to a gate or an entrance, while the 7–5–3 combination (j) and slab-and-stone combination II (h) are suitable for a stretch of open ground. Scale patterns I (m) and II (n) can be used across open ground. Scale pattern I (m) can also make a graceful curved path. Kobori Enshu made it famous, using it across sand in the garden at Konchi-in, Nanzen-ji Temple, Kyoto.

laid near the house where there might be some open ground; a stone of some height is usually provided as a step down from the verandah.

After the stepping-stones have been set in the ground, they can be surrounded by gravel or sand, or moss may be allowed to grow between them. For a more formal straight path, however, a combination of smaller stones with rectangular paving stones set in a geometrical pattern makes a very handsome alternative. This kind of paving is suitable for paths that will be in continual heavy use, and is therefore often employed for walks within temple and shrine compounds. It is ideal for paths leading up to the front door. It is rather like cobblestones, but the individual stones are flatter and therefore less painful for the ankles and the soles of the feet.

Where the stones are thick, they are set directly in mortar (I part cement to 2.5 to 3 parts sand) which has been spread on a bed of gravel. If they are thin, the bed of gravel is first set with concrete 10 cm (4 in) deep, on top of which the mortar is laid after the concrete has been allowed to dry for a day or two. When the stones are of both kinds, the thicker ones are set first, using the former technique, after which the remaining spaces are filled with the thinner kind, using the concrete method. This type of path looks striking when edged with gravel.

left: *Although pines and ever-greens form the backbone of most traditional Japanese gardens, maples are often used near paths for the pleasant dappled shade they give throughout the spring, summer, and autumn months. On a crisp autumn day drifts of crimson maple leaves, each starry shape distinct against a deep blue sky, look as though they are floating on water.*

facing page: *A traditional* roji, *or tea garden, helps to re-create the feeling of a rustic Japanese retreat in a mountain forest. The planting is very informal. The path picks its way through lush ferns and* Farfugium japonicum, *which help to reinforce the sense of seclusion and privacy. This garden belongs to the Tabuchi family of Ako, Japan.*

Bridges

Stepping-stones can be used across shallow running water for a naturalistic effect, but several kinds of bridges have traditionally been used for various kinds of formal gardens.

The humpback wooden bridge with vermilion-coloured railings is very well-known. It needs to be employed with caution lest the bright colour over-whelms everything else in the garden. It works best in large gardens, where it can be seen from a distance, its bold colour and shape softened by the planting of a delicate weeping willow or a Japanese maple by the foot of the bridge. In Japan these bridges were a part of the aristocratic gardens of the tenth and eleventh centuries, which were created around lakes and little islands. Keep the vermilion bridge for a special scenic spot in the garden.

Elegant wooden bridges, either humpbacked or straight, were used to connect islands in those aristo-cratic lake gardens of Kyoto, and in the hill-and-pond stroll gardens of later periods. They were often designed to produce a pleasing reflection in the deep water of the lake. Where the pond was planted with water irises, rushes and water-lilies, a zig-zag (*yatsuhashi*) bridge was a favourite. This type of bridge is still very popular; it is best described as a narrow boardwalk with wooden planks set out in a zig-zag pattern across the pond or a broad stream. Being a low bridge, it allows people to stroll literally among the plants growing in the water.

Types of humpback bridge other than the vermilion variety can be less obtrusive and overwhelming in a smaller garden. Made of either logs or wooden planks, and varnished to bring out the natural hue of the wood,

they can enhance the rustic feel of Japanese gardens. They can even be made of turf, supported on a tier of logs, then one of bamboo and finally a sheet of zinc. A turf bridge should not have railings. Generally speaking, short bridges look better if they do not have prominent high railings, though, of course, when planning a bridge, the safety of those using the garden must come first.

Whereas turf and other humpback bridges are par-ticularly good in gardens with dense, low ground-cover, simpler bridges are used in moss gardens and other types of dry-landscape gardens. These usually consist of nothing more than a long, flat slab of stone, set over the fine gravel, or bed of pebbles, symbolising the water.

A stone bridge usually has a pair of stones flanking it at both ends. The four stones should all be of different sizes and heights. Such stones are occasionally

seen in conjunction with wooden, as well as turf, bridges. Stone-slab bridges are also ideal for narrow streams in small-scale water gardens, where a wooden bridge with railings might look out of proportion. Two slabs of rock can be arranged end to end and supported in the middle by a tall boulder to form a single span over a slightly wider, shallow stream.

Stone bridges are traditionally used in front of waterfalls, whether dry or in full flow. They suited the

Zen Buddhist taste for rugged, austere representations of Nature in the garden, and were adopted in the intimate stroll gardens of Zen Buddhist temples. Single pieces of cut stone, often with a slight curve, are sometimes used instead of natural stone. These are now becoming available in the West as well, and they can be a very good alternative to naturally weathered rock, though their hard, straight lines give them a slightly artificial feel.

above: *A yatsuhashi* bridge is *extremely informal. The handrail does not extend along the whole length of the bridge, but only where the designer thinks someone might want to pause and take in the view.*

left: *This area of "An Oriental Garden", designed by NJ Landscapes for the Malvern Show, 1998, gives a good idea of the design of a yatsuhashi bridge, though this example is more ornamental than practical. The zig-zag design comes into its own when it is used to cross wide sections of shallow water or boggy or swampy land.*

above: *Choose a style of bridge that fits in with the overall character of your garden. A rustic bridge, such as this one, tends to suit a narrow or shallow stream better than a more ornate kind.*

Types of bridges

right: *A turf bridge is supported by a row of logs secured to two crosspieces which run the whole length of the bridge. A tier of bamboo canes is constructed on top of the row of logs. A sheet of thin metal supports the soil, which should be slightly banked up along the edges of the bridge. Lay turf so that its root system will hold the soil in place.*

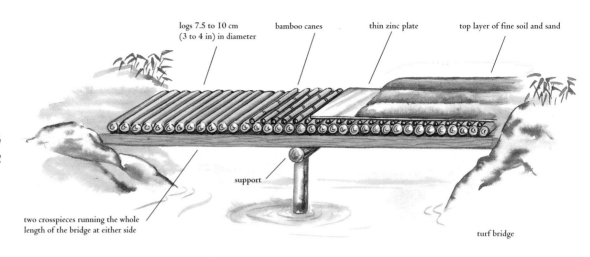

logs 7.5 to 10 cm (3 to 4 in) in diameter   bamboo canes   thin zinc plate   top layer of fine soil and sand

support

two crosspieces running the whole length of the bridge at either side

turf bridge

zig-zag (yatsuhashi) bridge I

left: *Zig-zag bridges are usually constructed of wooden planks, which are supported by horizontal struts held in place between two piles. It is important to make sure that bridges, if they are to be more than ornamental, are sturdy enough to bear the weight of humans. Professional advice from firms specializing in the construction of bridges is recommended.*

above: *A clever inversion has been used here: the moss represents the stream and the gravel dry land. Pine logs have been woven together with twine to construct a raft-like bridge. A structure of this kind forms the foundation of turf bridges. Chinese balloon flower (Platycodon grandiflorus) in very small, isolated clumps can be planted among moss to replicate how Iris laevigata would grow by a real stream.*

below: *The zig-zag pattern can be modified to suit a particular garden. This style is better than style I for crossings over shallow streams. It can also be built with cut stone. Cut-stone bridges are often used in tea gardens; single-span bridges of this type often have a slight curve to them. Being stone bridges, they are usually flanked by a pair of rocks of differing heights at either end.*

zig-zag (yatsuhashi) bridge II

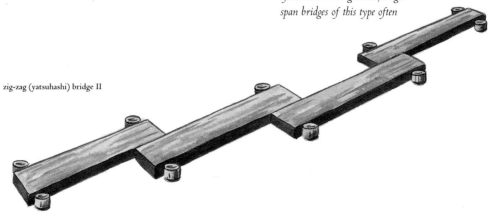

left: *A short* yatsuhashi-*type bridge can be made with stone slabs instead of wooden planks. Cut stones will produce a more geometric effect, but naturally shaped slabs can look very attractive and interesting. This example is from a New England garden, designed and owned by Fred Watson.*

Stone lanterns

right: *The original of this famous* kotoji *lantern used over water is found at Kenroku-en Park in the city of Kanazawa on the Sea of Japan. Its shape is like the struts supporting the strings on a* koto, *a Japanese zither.*

below: *There are four types of stone lanterns: the* oki-gata, *which sits on a flat rock (a); the* tachi-gata, *the most traditional type of lantern, originally from shrines and temples (b); the* ikegomi-gata *(c), which has its shaft stuck in the ground; and lanterns with legs (d), which look good among low, round shrubs near water.*

Votive stone lanterns have always embellished roads and paths leading to Shinto shrines and Buddhist temples. They combined utility with beauty and were often donated by the faithful. On certain ceremonial days, many of these lanterns are still lighted with tiny candles, the windows screened with rice-paper; they illuminate the way for worshippers attending an evening rite.

Lanterns were brought into the garden in the sixteenth century with the development of the tea garden. Although the greatest of all tea masters, Sen-no-Rikyu, is said to have introduced them into his tea gardens because he admired the distant flicker of their light, lanterns served the dual purposes of ornamenting the garden and guiding guests on their way to an evening tea ceremony. Nowadays they are more often decorative, but they should be positioned with their original purpose in mind. They can, for instance, be placed near a *tsukubai*, if the basin does not possess a stone for a hand-held lantern.

There are four main types of stone lantern and their uses differ slightly. The standard lantern has both a shaft and a pedestal. This is known as the *tachi-gata*, or standing lantern. Many of these are named after ancient temples, where their prototypes are still found. The best-known is the six-sided lantern found at, and named after, the Kasuga Shrine in Nara. These lanterns tend to be large and elaborately carved, making them rather ponderous. Still, they have dignity and poise, and they can be imposing when placed near paths, gates or entrances, or against tall shrubbery. They can be complemented

with a pine tree, *Ilex integra, I. crenata* (box-leaved holly), *Ternstroemia gymnanthera, Taxus cuspidata* (Japanese yew), *Torreya nucifera* (Japanese nutmeg yew) or *Viburnum japonicum*. The elegance of Japanese maples, *Ilex serrata* (Japanese winterberry) and *Euonymus alatus* (winged euonymus) creates a pleasing contrast to the gravity of this type of lantern.

A more modest type of lantern lacks the pedestal. Called *ikegomi-gata*, these lanterns are stuck straight into the ground. They look effective against less dense planting in the inner or courtyard garden. They also show up well against gravel and sand; their simpler form suits a more austere atmosphere. The appealing simplicity of their shape makes them appropriate for tea gardens as well, and for use next to low stone basins. The most famous design of this kind is the *oribe-gata*, easily recognized by the round bulge on its shaft.

The third type, the *oki-gata*, lacks the shaft. These are placed on flat stones. In wet and dry gardens

alike, a lantern of this type standing, or rather sitting, on a piece of land jutting out into the water produces a pleasing illusion of a lighthouse perched on a promontory.

The last type of lantern has legs. It can be octagonal, hexagonal or circular in shape and can have two, three, four or more legs. The best-known is the *yukimi-gata*, particularly attractive when seen in snow. Shorter and more compact than lanterns with shafts, they are also excellent for use next to water.

Other kinds of lanterns have one or more long, curved shafts. These are used specifically to lean over water. There are also rectangular stone lanterns in the shape of old-fashioned Japanese road signs

(*michi-shirube*); the light is placed behind a lattice window at the top. These should be placed at intervals along a path. Another variety is the pagoda, which can have between three and eleven tiers, so long as it is an odd number. Pagodas are available in different styles, some with hardly any space between the tiered roofs; these are more in the native style than those with ornamented windows, which are pseudo-Chinese. The best place to put a tall pagoda is up a slope in a far corner of the garden, where it will be very effective in creating the illusion of distance. In a flat garden, a bulky pagoda needs tall, slender trees and dense shrubs around it so that it does not look too bare and exposed.

above: *A round oki-gata lantern is typically placed at the end of a pebbly spit of land jutting out into water. One of the most important examples in Japan can be seen at the Katsura Imperial Villa outside Kyoto. The effect can be re-created in very restricted spaces as it works equally well in dry-landscape gardens. This example is in a garden in Augsburg, Germany.*

Pergolas

right: *In Japan, wisteria trellises have traditionally been constructed using stout bamboo poles bound together with black hemp-palm rope.*

The graceful, lavender-purple racemes of wisteria have an Edwardian elegance about them when draped over pale stone or red brick. These days, the idea of growing wisteria as a standard has also become widely accepted in the West. Indeed, surprisingly enough, wisteria can flower happily in a large pot as long as it is carefully pruned so that it does not outgrow the restricted amount of nutrient available.

In Japan, wisteria is generally trained carefully along a pergola. This is ideal for *Wisteria floribunda* (Japanese wisteria), as its racemes can be up to 60 cm (2 ft) long. *Wisteria chinensis* produces slightly shorter racemes of between 20 and 30 cm (8 to 12 in). In early summer, the pergola becomes a canopy of cascading blooms. There are very old and famous wisterias trained in this fashion all over Japan, and pergolas of this type hold a place of distinction in the garden. They should never have to compete for attention. They are given pride of place, uncrowded by other plants, perhaps set against a sedate, deep green backdrop of shapely pines. The trunk is also considered a beautiful asset of the plant – the more so the older the plant. Wisteria is planted against a pergola in such a way that the shape of the entire plant can be seen and admired when in flower and even when it is not. The wisteria is often surrounded by clean, white gravel, accompanied by a simple seat under the pergola. This seat, with no back or armrests, will be a simple slab of stone or a cross-section of a tree-trunk, highly polished so its age rings gleam.

For the posts and cross-beams of the pergola, *hinoki* cypress logs are generally used. They are treated with creosote or a similar preservative to stop them rotting – traditionally, the surface of the wood was charred, then brought to a high polish. Using poles for this frame rather than sawn timber creates a more rustic look, and is preferable for smaller pergolas holding one or two plants. The posts are connected to each other at the top with cross-beams. The pergola should be at least 2.5 m (8 ft 2 in) high.

The bamboo trellis secured to the top of this wooden frame is characteristic of Japanese-style pergolas. The trellis is composed of vertical and horizontal canes of bamboo, 5 cm (2 in) or slightly less in diameter and secured with wire, which are placed at 30 cm (1 ft) – occasionally up to 45 cm (1 ft 6 in) – intervals to form a lattice pattern. Using bamboo that is too thick will make the pergola seem top-heavy. Usually a space covering six or seven canes

– about 2 m (6 ft 7 in) – is allowed between two supporting wooden posts. The trellis should extend beyond the end of the wooden cross-pieces by the length of one interval between canes.

The overall impression should be one of lightness, but the pergola must be sturdy enough to bear the considerable weight of fully-grown wisterias.

Wisteria tends to take a long time to bloom, although "Issai" varieties flower sooner than more traditional ones. From spring onwards, wisteria produces long shoots, which should be cut back late in summer. Leave some of them in the first two years to cover the trellis. In January or February these shoots are pruned back to between 30 cm and I m (I ft to 3 ft 4 in). The plant then produces short spurs with flower-buds.

above: *Here, a wisteria in full bloom forms a dramatic entrance to the oriental section of the garden. Wisteria pergolas can serve as delightful, informal arbours. A pergola is also an effective way of presenting certain kinds of specimen plants in a large garden.*

Fences

Fences become a prominent feature of a garden the smaller it is. In keeping with other features of the Japanese-style garden, natural materials are always preferable to artificial ones. The most important of these is, unsurprisingly, bamboo. Many varieties of bamboo are harvested for various purposes in Japan, therefore it can be obtained in different thicknesses. Thicker grades of bamboo up to 15 cm (6 in) across are becoming available in the West as well. Bamboo fences are meant to be impermanent; they are allowed to weather and are replaced every five years or so.

Another characteristic of Japanese garden fences is that the use of nails is avoided as much as possible. The fences are usually woven, or bound together using a rope traditionally made of hemp-palm fibre. This rope is black, and gives distinctive touches of colour to these fences.

Bamboo fences can either be open-weave or close-weave; the choice of style depends on how much privacy is desired. Open-weave fences tend to be short, and they are used to mark off planted areas in the garden. The basic fence of this type is the *yotsume*, or four-eyed fence, composed of interwoven horizontal and vertical poles. The *kinkakuji* fence, named after the famous Golden Pavilion Temple in Kyoto, has a similar square weave, but it is distinguished by being crowned with split bamboo. The *yarai* and *ryoanji* styles are both diagonal weaves, the latter again having a split bamboo top.

The close-weave fence obviously gives more privacy than the open-weave types. It is as good as a screen, and is used, often in combination with rows

of tall conifers or evergreens, to mark the outer boundaries of a large garden. It may not be possible then to appreciate the fence from the house, but this kind of fence, being very elegant and decorative, may be one of the least ugly or offensive ways of putting up a high barrier between private property and a public road. Sometimes a close-weave fence is placed in front of tall trees or shrubs in such a way that their upper branches can still be seen above it. Overhanging branches can help to soften the austere straight lines of this type of fence. They are particularly attractive if the trees are flowering ones. If a bough leans into a garden, the fence is simply built round it.

The *kenninji* fence is one of the most frequently seen. It is a high fence of split bamboo woven closely together in a single row along horizontal struts, which are thick bamboo canes split in half. These struts, which can be either four or five in number

right: *The slender grace of bamboo is brought out by the Japanese custom of carefully removing the lower branches from cultivated bamboo. This produces the special cool serenity of a bamboo grove or forest. The bushy leaves high overhead form a canopy that shuts out the remorseless summer sun, and everything below is still and calm in an eerie green light.*

facing page: *Branches of* kuromoji *(Japanese spicebush) form a choice material for rustic-style fences (see also page 128). The lacquered reddish-black tone of their bark lends particular elegance to a country garden. The branches have been patiently arranged back to front and in overlapping rows secured with horizontal bamboo struts.*

(four is common in the west of Japan and five in the east) form the back of the fence. Halved lengths of bamboo are also set horizontally along the front of the fence to hide the rope-work that holds it together. These struts, unlike those at the back, are meant to be ornamental and are secured to the fence with neat knots at wide but regular intervals. For a greater degree of formality, the top of the fence can be covered with more horizontal pieces of bamboo, but this is not necessary in an informal setting, provided that the top of the fence is trimmed straight. The *kenninji* fence should not have any gaps between the vertical shafts of bamboo. It is used most often as a perimeter fence, but a short length of it is also useful as a way of defining separate areas within a garden.

The *kenninji* fence is sometimes mounted on a low stone wall. This combination is called a *ginkakuji* fence, and it is particularly imposing when set against a tall, pruned conifer hedge, as it is along the entrance path to the Silver Pavilion Temple in Kyoto, after which it is named. Sometimes, thinner types of bamboo are used for the vertical pieces, in which case the fence is known as the *shimizu* style. *Takeho* fences specifically use sheaves of bamboo branches instead, *kuromoji* fences use the branches of the Japanese spicebush (*Lindera umbellata*) and *hagi* fences are made with the slender branches of the Japanese bush clover (*Lespedeza* species). These brushwood or reed fences have a delightful rustic elegance about them, especially when the material is a different colour from the bamboo; Japanese spicebush (*kuromoji*), for example, has rich reddish-brown bark. The straighter and more even in quality the brushwood is, the smoother the surface of the finished fence will be. Often this kind of fence looks as though it has been beautifully combed into place, though it is sometimes intentionally made with coarser material for an even more countrified look. While brushwood has an attractive

delicacy, the fence itself should look quite solid. Occasionally, the thinner material is used for the horizontal pieces instead; this style of fence draws people's attention to the thick canes of bamboo used

vertically, so it tends to emphasize the height of the fence rather than its length.

A popular way of using fences in Japan is not to take them from one end of a garden to the other, but to use them as a short screen or blind. The smallest gardens often have a high, narrow fence built at a right angle to the house, forming a sheltering windbreak near a doorway. These fences are called *sode-gaki*, or sleeve fences, and they are also useful for partly screening off sections of a garden. Any kind of weave, whether open or closed, formal or rustic, can be used for a sleeve fence, depending on its

above: *Branches of bamboo have been used to produce this sleeve fence (see also page 128). It is placed beside an entrance to screen part of the front of a building from view. Although rustic in style, it is tidy enough for a formal position. A huge cluster of bamboo branches decorates the end of the fence.*

facing page: *The* kenninji *fence (see also page 128) is the most common style of bamboo fence used for screening off areas around the house and garden.*

Constructing bamboo fences

method A		method B		method C

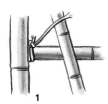

1

Kenninji fences: *Of the two methods for securing split bamboo along a horizontal strut with a continuous length of rope, (A) is less decorative, and the rope-work can later be hidden behind ornamental struts of halved canes of bamboo fastened to the fence, using the knot illustrated on the far right (C).*

The second method (B) produces an attractive pattern for kenninji-style fences (such as the one on page 126).

1

Yotsume and teppo fences: The diagram on the right (C) shows the basic method for tying bamboo canes together for yotsume and teppo fences. Yotsume fences (shown on pages 31 and 75, bottom right) have vertical canes which are arranged alternately on the front and back of the horizontal struts, which can be either three or four in number. Patterns can be created, for instance, using two vertical canes together at set intervals.

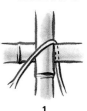

1

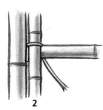

2

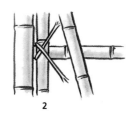

2

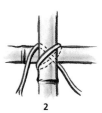

2

Brushwood fences: *This type of fence, shown on pages 125 and 127, is constructed by building up several rows of brushwood, held securely in place between horizontal struts of thin split bamboo. The brushwood is made to stand upright by tying the two horizontal struts together at regular intervals. First the back of the fence is constructed like this; then the horizontal struts are slightly loosened and another row of brushwood is inserted to create the front.*

Teppo fences (such as the one shown on page 58) are constructed in the same way, but with no space left between the vertical canes. Being screen fences, they are double the height of yotsume fences. Often they have alternating groups of five and three canes, the former placed in front of the horizontal struts and the latter behind.

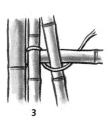

3

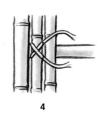

3

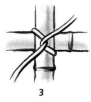

3

(seen from the back)

4

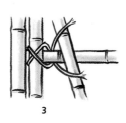

4

Once a row is completed both back and front, halved canes of bamboo are clamped over the horizontal struts on either side of the fence. These canes are tightly fastened using individual, ornamental knots (C). The tips of the brushwood (which will be facing outwards on either side of the fence) are all neatly tucked into the fence. A beginner can use wire mesh to support the fence, but it is important to build up both sides of the fence so that the wire does not show.

The number of horizontal struts can differ according to the taste of the garden designer. They can be evenly spaced from top to bottom of the fence, or they can be divided into two groups of either two or three struts each. One group can be placed towards the top and the other towards the bottom of the fence, leaving the centre of the fence clear and emphasizing its height.

4

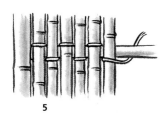

5

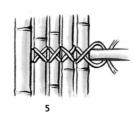

5

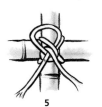

5

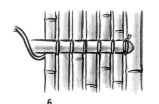

6

(seen from the back)

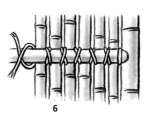

6

(seen from the back)

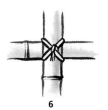

6

intended purpose and the general style of the garden. One famous kind, which is known as the *koetsuji* fence (named after yet another Kyoto temple), is long and narrow, and tapers towards the end in a distinctive curve. It is basically a *yarai*-style fence crowned with a thick sheaf of bamboo branches and thinly split bamboo. It is often used as a backdrop for a mossy stone-and-sand garden, to separate it from the rest of a larger garden. The *koetsuji* fence is effective when used against low-growing, formally pruned shrubs like azaleas, and ground-hugging plants.

The thicker and straighter the bamboo is, the more formal the fence will appear. Brushwood fences, on the other hand, can be constructed of locally available materials such as hazel, wattle or willow branches. Make friends with the people who coppice any nearby woods. Coarser, uneven branches can still be turned into a good fence with character, but it is important to remember that any one type of material used should all be of the same thickness and quality.

Garden walls in Japan were traditionally made of wattle and daub and were often whitewashed. Such walls serve as the background to some of the most famous Zen temple gardens of rocks and gravel, their whiteness mirroring the whiteness of the gravel. Pruned evergreens also look particularly fine silhouetted against a white wall. The choice of a fence or garden wall and the material of which it is made depends ultimately on the general formality of the entire garden. A rustic fence of brushwood may be suitable for part of a tea garden, while it would look too crude in an abstract dry-landscape garden of rocks and gravel. Some garden suppliers in the West stock woven wicker fences and screens made of split bamboo, heather, coppiced willow, reeds or other material. These may be too flimsy for most Japanese gardens, though it might be possible to give extra support to screens of this kind by adding horizontal

struts of thick, straight bamboo. The function of fences and walls in Japanese gardens is not simply to establish boundaries, for they help to draw the eye to the landscape beyond. The height of the fence should harmonize with plants both inside and beyond the partition. Fences thus help to create a sense of space rather than that of confinement.

above: *An original bamboo screen design by Robert Ketchell and Eileen Tunnell for the "Ox-herding Pictures" Garden at the Hampton Court Flower Show in 1996.*

Borrowed vistas

This idea, of course, is by no means unique to Japanese gardens. If you have a garden that looks out towards a splendid distant vista, make the most of it by incorporating the view into the overall garden design. Don't hide it behind a dense hedge of Leyland cypress!

Fences, garden walls and hedges in Japanese gardens do not shut the garden in by shutting the external world out. Bamboo fences meant primarily for screening purposes are often built incorporating an open weave along the top to draw the eye to the landscape beyond. A rectilinear, dry-landscape Zen temple garden of the most austere kind is often surrounded by a whitewashed mud wall, which creates the feeling of an enclosed, self-sufficient world. But a row of majestic firs or cypresses beyond the garden wall not only helps to soften the stern line of the wall by drawing the eye upwards toward the sky; it also connects the garden with the vista that unfolds in the distance. At Entsu-ji Temple in Kyoto, columnar *hinoki* cypresses frame the distant view of Mount Hiei, grey like an ink painting on silk. A view of a shapely mountain is greatly esteemed in Japan for its spiritual and aesthetic resonance. At Shoden-ji Temple, also in Kyoto, the view of eastern mountains is echoed in the pruned azaleas in its dry-landscape garden.

In this way the garden is seen to mirror Nature and Nature seems to mirror the garden. This is the ultimate aim of the Japanese garden. It is a microcosm created to nestle within the macrocosm of the natural world, a segment of Nature as well as a work of art.

right: *The Max Koch Garden in Switzerland, designed by Anthony Paul, modifies the stone-slab type of foot-bridge to suit a location much more open than a typical Japanese landscape. Since there are few trees, the distant view of the mountains is not obscured and the feeling of wide open space is preserved. At the same time, the tall, stiff leaves of the water irises (*Iris laevigata*) and the flower spikes of the water plantain (*Alisma plantago-aquatica*) give a sense of height to the garden.*

CHAPTER THREE

Plant Directory

The serenity of Japanese gardens comes from making careful designs seem utterly natural and unobtrusive. Clipped evergreens and pruned conifers serve as the backdrop for seasonal displays of fragile flowers. Japanese apricots and *Cornus officinalis* bloom in earliest spring. Azaleas such as *Rhododendron quinquefolium* and *R. reticulatum* create a haze of colour at the height of spring, while summer brings the cool white blossoms of *Cornus kousa*, *Stewartia pseudocamellia*, or *Styrax japonicus*. A clump of "wild" flowers – balloon flowers, *Aster tartaricus* or toad lilies – signals the coming of autumn. The rustling of tall flower-heads of *Miscanthus sinensis* warns that frosts to redden the leaves of the maples will not be long. The bright red berries of *Ardisia crenata* decorate the garden through the cold winter months.

Understatement, rather than profusion, creates the calmness of this style of gardening.

Trees

Coniferous trees

Chamaecyparis obtusa var. *breviramea* (chabo-hiba/ Kamakura-hiba): a dwarf form of the Japanese hinoki cypress, often seen in gardens in Japan, but other dwarf cultivars of *C. obtusa* are also available; prune, if necessary to maintain shape, late winter- early spring; hardy to USDA zone 5.

Chamaecyparis pisifera "Plumosa" (nikko-hiba/ shinobu-hiba): a dwarf garden cultivar of the Japanese sawara cypress; tolerant of hard pruning; used for topiary and hedges; drooping branches and scale-like leaves; USDA hardiness zones 4 through 8; slow-growing; moist, non-alkaline soil; full sun to partial shade; do not let its roots dry out; when pruning, take care not to cut back to old wood; *C. p.* "Filifera" (ito-hiba, hiyoku-hiba) has very fine foliage, and grows to 2 m (6 ft 7 in) in height; will not grow in shade.

Cryptomeria japonica (Japanese cedar; sugi): 25 x 6 m (82 x 20 ft); columnar in shape; USDA hardiness zones 6 through 8; needs moisture and good drainage; sun; fast-growing; hates pollution; good as a background or screen; "Elegans Compacta" (2 m (6 ft 7 in) high) has green foliage that goes bronze in winter.

Juniperus chinensis "Kaizuka" (kaizuka-ibuki): 6 x 4 m (19 ft 6 in x 13 ft); USDA hardiness zones 4 through 9; well-drained soil, preferably sandy; tolerates drought; dislikes wet soil; sun; stop central leader to restrict height and encourage lateral branches for a denser appearance; clip to establish desired shape but lightly prune to maintain size thereafter by cutting back spurs shorter than outline of tree in autumn; tolerates pollution; dislikes root disturbance; suitable for planting in rows or as broad, pruned hedges; cultivars in various sizes and with different habits available, ranging from large trees to shrubs and low groundcover.

Juniperus conferta (shore juniper; hainezu): a dense evergreen shrub found along sand dunes and rocky seashores in Japan; shade tolerant, tolerant of sea spray as well as dry conditions; sharp needles; spreading growth to 1 to 1.5m (3 to 4ft) and to approx 30cm (1ft) in height; USDA hardiness zones 6 through 9; recommended cultivars include "Silver Mist", "Blue Pacific", "All Gold" and "Emerald Sea".

Pinus densiflora (Japanese red pine; aka-matsu): 15 x 7 m (50 x 23 ft); conical, becoming flat- topped; USDA hardiness zones 3 through 7; dry conditions; can be pruned; very intolerant of air pollution; *P. densiflora* "Umbraculifera" (tagyosho) is a multi-trunked garden cultivar which eventually forms a broad, rounded umbrella crown; "Umbraculifera Nana" grows to 2m or 6ft.

Pinus parviflora (Japanese white pine; goyo- matsu): conical; 10 x 8 m (32 ft 6 in x 26 ft); USDA hardiness zones 5 through 7.

Pinus thunbergii (Japanese black pine; kuro- matsu): 15 x 6 m (49 x 19 ft 6 in); USDA hardiness zones 5 through 8.

Podocarpus macrophyllus (yew pine/yew plum pine/Buddhist pine; kusa-maki/inu-maki): 15 x 8 m (49 x 19 ft 6 in); USDA hardiness zones 7 through 9; frost hardy; conical with yew-like leaves; dislikes wet; fast-growing in warmer zones, needing summer humidity and heat to reach full height, otherwise it remains a shrub; can tolerate shade; *P. m.* var. *maki* (arhat pine; rakan-maki) is a much- prized variety with smaller leaves; rich, slightly acid, moist but well-drained soil; prune, if necessary early summer or mid-autumn; can be used for hedges.

Sciadopitys verticillata (Japanese umbrella pine; koya-maki): 10 x 6 m (32 ft 6 in x 19 ft 6 in); USDA hardiness zones 5 through 8; rich, moist, well-drained, neutral to slightly acid soil; full sun to partial shade; slow-growing and compact; peeling reddish bark; dislikes pollution; resents root disturbance; can be planted in groups; dwarf and pendulous cultivars also available.

Taxus cuspidata (Japanese yew; ichii/araragi/ onko): 15 to 20 m (49 to 65 ft); USDA hardiness zones 4 through 7; tolerates shade; needs moisture in autumn but dislikes wet; will not tolerate poor drainage; resents root disturbance; shelter from dry, cold winter winds; red fruits in autumn on female plants; peeling bark on older plants; prune twice a year in early summer and early autumn; old wood will not produce new buds; *Taxus cuspidata* var. *nana* (kyaraboku) is shorter and forms a round shape, 2 to 4 m (6 ft 7 in to 13 ft); "Densa" is a shorter, female shrub, 1.2 m (4 ft).

Thujopsis dolabrata (hiba arborvitae; asunaro/ hiba): up to 15 m (49 ft); USDA hardiness zones 5 through 7; conical; scale-like leaves; avoid strongly alkaline soils; likes moist, well-drained conditions; will not produce new shoots from branches more than three or four years old; start pruning early if a small shrub is wanted; prune at start of spring and autumn, picking off tips of shoots; "Nana" is a dwarf cultivar.

Torreya nucifera (Japanese nutmeg yew; kaya): 15 x 8 m (49 x 26 ft); USDA hardiness zones 6 through 10; slow growing; conical; sun or dappled shade; needs hot, humid summers to do well; good for south-eastern US, northern New Zealand, south-eastern Australia; slightly acidic, rich and moist but well-drained soil; edible seeds but not self-fertile; traditionally used in Japan for wood- working.

Evergreen trees

Buxus microphylla var. *japonica* (Japanese box; tsuge): up to 5 m (16 ft 3 in); USDA hardiness zones 6 through 9; half-shade; growth very slow; care needed in transplanting; likes lime; mulch to prevent shallow roots from drying out; wood used for making combs.

Cleyera japonica (sakaki): 3 x 3 m (10 x 10 ft); USDA hardiness zones 7 through 8, warmer areas of zone 6; rich, deep, acid soil; shade; can be pruned hard for broad hedges; use as underplant- ing; a tea-garden plant, also used around shrines.

Daphniphyllum macropodum (yuzuriha): to 15 m (49 ft); USDA hardiness zones 7 through 9; frost hardy; a round shrub or tree; rich soil; half-shade; no pruning needed; leaves in whorls, which droop as new leaves appear; used for New Year's decorations; mass planting; suitable for north-facing gardens.

Dendropanax trifidus (kakure-mino): 10 m (32 ft 6 in); USDA hardiness zones 7 through 9; frost hardy; moist shade; very slow-growing; dislikes being pruned; resents root disturbance; suitable for north- facing gardens; used around shrines and in tea gardens.

Ilex crenata (box-leaved holly/Japanese holly; inu-tsuge): 5 x 4 m (16 ft 3 in x 13 ft); USDA hardiness zones 6 through 9; small, round, glossy leaves; partial shade; moist conditions; important for topiary in Japan; slow-growing but vigorous; avoid winter wind; if soil is alkaline, give an annual feed of acid fertilizer.

Ilex integra (mochi-no-ki): 7 to 8 m (23 to 26 ft); USDA hardiness zones 8 through 9; young plants tend to by half hardy, but established plants can tolerate temperatures down to -10°C/14°F; moist, rich soil; sun; slow-growing; prune heavily in early summer by trimming back branches to two or three new leaves; can be transplanted even when quite big; used near shrines.

Ilex latifolia (luster-leaf holly; tarayo): large, serrated leathery leaves; male and female plants necessary for production of the attractive red berries; height 6 to 7.5m (20 to 25ft), but can be hard pruned or clipped to create a dense screen if grown in

full sun (produces more open growth if grown in shade); best pruned late winter-early spring; multi-trunked specimens also sometimes available; USDA hardiness zones 7 through 9; frost hardy.

Ilex pedunculosa (long-stalk holly; soyogo): upright habit to 6m (20ft) in height; USDA zone 5; prefers moist, slightly acidic, well-drained soil in full sun to partial shade; tolerant of air pollution; also has some sea-air tolerance; useful as a screen; both male and female plants needed for the red autumn berries.

Ilex rotunda (kurogane holly/ round-leaf holly; kurogane-mochi): a slow-growing evergreen which can eventually reach 9 to 15m (30 to 50ft) in height; stop central leader once desired height is reached; reduce number of lateral branches if a "cloud"- pruned topiary style is desired; prune lightly Nov-Dec, then prune hard and shape late spring; female plants produce attractive red berries during the winter; popular plant for bonsai; tolerates partial shade; USDA hardiness zones 6 through 9.

Lithocarpus edulis (Japanese stone oak; mate-bashii): 10 m (32 ft 6 in); USDA hardiness zones 7 through 9; hardy in the southern half of the UK; sun or partial shade; fast-growing; tolerates heavy pruning; for hedging or mass planting.

Pittosporum tobira (Japanese mock orange; tobera): a rounded, dense evergreen growing anywhere from 2 to 9m (6 to 30ft) in height; leathery leaves; clusters of fragrant white flowers in late spring to early summer; seed capsules produce red seeds in winter; male and female plants required for seeds; tolerant of sea air and some dryness; leaves and branches emit a strong smell when crushed; no pruning required; USDA hardiness zones 8 through 11; half hardy; cultivars with variegated leaves available.

Osmanthus x fortunei (Fortune's osmanthus; hiiragi-mokusei: *O. fragrans x O. heterophyllus*): 5 m (16 ft 3 in); USDA hardiness zones 7 through 9; frost hardy; upright; holly-like, glossy green leaves; half-shade or complete shade; prune; tolerant of sea air; suitable for hedges and planting in rows; fragrant tubular white flowers in late summer to autumn; likes slightly acid soil.

Osmanthus heterophyllus (holly osmanthus/holly olive/false holly/Chinese holly; hiiragi): 4 to 8 m (13 to 26 ft); USDA hardiness zones 7 through 9; frost hardy; holly-like, spiny, leathery leaves; tolerates shade; slowly forms a dense round shrub; can be pruned; tolerates sea air; can be grown alone, but also suitable for hedges; fragrant, white tubular flowers on female plants in late autumn, berries mature by the following summer.

Quercus glauca (ring-cup oak/Japanese blue oak/glaucous-leaf oak; ara-kashi): a slow-growing live oak (evergreen) which can eventually attain 9m (30ft); serrated lance-shaped leaves purple-crimson

in colour when young, turning glossy green above and glaucous blue-green underneath; somewhat coarser leaves than *Q. myrsinifolia*; good for hedges, windbreaks, screens; USDA hardiness zones 7 through 9; frost hardy.

Quercus myrsinifolia (bamboo-leaf oak/Chinese evergreen oak/Chinese ring-cupped oak; shira-kashi): a slow-growing live oak (evergreen) with glossy lance-shaped leaves emerging bronze-red; can grow to 6 to 12m (20 to 40ft), but close planting, as for a hedge, will reduce vigour; plant shrubs 30cm (12in) apart for a 1m(3ft)-tall hedge, 50cm (20in) apart for a 1.5m (5ft)-tall hedge; stop central leader when preferred height is reached; prune for a dense hedge in July and November; traditionally used as windbreaks in central Japan; shade tolerant; USDA hardiness zones 7 through 9; frost hardy.

Quercus phillyraeoides (ubame-gashi): a slow-growing, dense live oak (evergreen), with glossy ovate leaves and fissured brown-grey bark; suitable for hedges; stop main leading stem at required height and cut back lateral branches to desired length; prune late autumn; can grow to 6 to 9m (20-30ft) in height; acid to neutral soil; USDA hardiness zones 7 through 10.

Ternstroemia gymnanthera (mokkoku): 5 to 10 m (16 to 32 ft 6 in); USDA hardiness zones 7 through 10; frost hardy to half hardy in the UK; usually dislikes temperatures below -5°C/23°F; ripe wood tolerates colder conditions; partial or complete shade; rich acid soil; in early summer remove the longest central stem from each new growth.

Deciduous trees

Acer buergerianum (three-toothed maple/trident maple; to-kaede): broad leaves with three triangular lobes, dark green above and blue-green on the underside, turning orange and red in the autumn; best in full sun; to 6 to 9m (20 to 30ft) in height; USDA hardiness zones 5 through 9.

Acer capillipes (snake-bark maple; hosoe-kaede): distinctive arching branches, green in colour with white streaks; often multi-trunked; serrated three-lobed leaves with prominent central lobe; red leaf stalks; to 9 to 12m (30 to 40ft) in height; USDA hardiness zones 5 through 7.

Acer cissifolium (ivy-leaved maple/ash-leaved maple; mitsude-kaede): a native of Japan producing deeply toothed, pointed trifoliate leaves opening bronze, later turning dark green and finally red in the autumn; best in partial shade and moist acidic soils; to 7m (25ft); USDA hardiness zones 5 through 8.

Acer japonicum (full moon maple; ha-uchiwa-kaede): USDA hardiness zones 5 through 7; tolerant of partial shade; slow-growing; acid soil; dislikes salt air; rounded leaves, seven to thirteen

shallowly toothed lobes, turning yellow and red in autumn; better than *A. palmatum* in heavy or alkaline soils; can be grown in a multi-trunk form.

Acer maximowiczianum (syn. *Acer nikoense*; Nikko maple; megusuri-no-ki): a slow-growing, rounded maple producing long, oval, slightly toothed, trifoliate leaves turning red in the autumn; best in partial shade; to 12m (40ft); USDA hardiness zones 5 through 7.

Acer mono (painted maple; itaya-kaede): broad, rounded leaves with five to seven tapered lobes; best in moist but well-drained acidic soil and partial shade; to 12m (40ft); USDA hardiness zones 5 through 8.

Acer palmatum (iroha-momiji/takao-kaede/momiji): many variations in leaf shape and colour which can change from spring through to autumn; USDA hardiness zones 5 through 8; vulnerable to early spring frosts; rich, deep, acid soil that does not dry out; sun (but some paler varieties may be scorched in hot sun); do not prune tips of branches; cut back overlong spurs and crowded branches at base; if the size of the plant needs to be reduced, cut back long branches to the next fork; has a very short dormant period so prune in late autumn, early winter; good for planting by edge of ponds and near lanterns; mulch with leaf mould in autumn and early spring; *A. p.* var. *heptalobum* has leaves with between five and seven lobes, turning a rich orange and red colour in the autumn; *A. p.* var. *matsumurae* (yama-momiji) has bigger leaves which are toothed; "Osakazuki" has a classical seven-lobed leaf-shape and orange-red autumn colour; "Sango-kaku" produces vibrant yellow autumn leaves and brilliant red branches which look lacquered; "Shindeshojo" and "Beni-tsukasa" also have very good leaf shapes; the "Dissectum" group has deeply divided, frond-like leaves.

Acer rufinerve (grey snake-bark maple/red-vein maple/Honshu maple; urihada-kaede): a small- to medium-sized tree with loosely three-lobed leaves, the central lobe being the largest; arching branches and striking bark, green with dark streaks when young, turning grey-brown and mottled as the tree ages; leaves change colour relatively later than other Japanese maples; height to 7 to 14m (25 to 45ft); USDA hardiness zones 6 through 8.

Acer shirasawanum "Aureum" (syn. *A. japonicum* "Aureum"; golden full-moon maple/golden shirasawa maple; o-itaya-meigetsu): bright yellow

facing page, from top left:
Blossoms on a Japanese apricot, traditionally known outside Japan as the Japanese plum (Prunus mume)
Autumn leaves on Zelkova serrata
Ardisia crenata
Saxifraga stolonifera *in October*

leaves with seven to eleven lobes, turning red in autumn; to 6m (20ft); USDA hardiness zones 5 through 7.

Acer sieboldianum (ko-uchiwa-kaede): rounded leaves with seven to eleven lobes similar to those of *A. japonicum*; small, upright habit; can be grown as a single-trunked specimen tree or in a multi-trunk shrub-like form; to 4.5m (15ft); USDA hardiness zones 5 through 8.

Carpinus laxiflora (loose-flowered hornbeam; akashide/soro): to 9m (30ft) in height, but also used for bonsai; small, oval, serrated leaves opening purple and later becoming green; good autumn colour; striped patterning on bark and reddish stems; moist, acidic, well-drained soil in sun or partial shade; hardy to USDA zone 6.

Cercidiphyllum japonicum (katsura): to 25 m (81 ft); USDA hardiness zones 5 through 8, warmer areas of zone 4; moist, rich, neutral to acid soil; sun, half-shade; can be pruned anytime apart from spring; reduce height and size by stopping central leader and reducing number of lateral branches; brilliant scarlet autumn colour (best in acid soil); var. *magnificum* shorter (to 10 m (32 ft 6 in)) with larger leaves; f. *pendulum* has a weeping habit.

Euonymus hamiltonianus subsp. *sieboldianus* (spindle tree; mayumi): 5 m (16 ft); USDA hardiness zones 4 through 8; fast-growing; sun; four-lobed pinkish-red fruits split to reveal red seeds on female plants in autumn; pruning not necessary but can be done during the winter to maintain a natural shape, removing long or weak branches and suckers at base; flowers form on short branches; autumn colour; good substitute for *E. alatus*, which has become invasive in the eastern United States.

Ginkgo biloba (maidenhair tree; icho): to 30 m (97 ft); USDA hardiness zones 3 through 8; upright; slow-growing; needs sun; flat, fan-like leaves turn brilliant yellow in autumn; tolerates drought and pollution; dioecious; trees grown in West tend to be male, but in Japan the nuts are eaten.

Poncirus trifoliata (hardy orange/trifoliate orange/Japanese bitter orange; karatachi): 2 to 3 m (6 ft 7 in to 10 ft); USDA hardiness zones 5 through 9; tolerant of partial shade, but prefers sun; dislikes root disturbance; fragrant five-petalled flowers in spring before leaves; inedible fruit like small oranges; very sharp spines on branches; used for tall, thick hedges.

Quercus serrata (Korean oak; ko-nara): an elegant deciduous oak with attractive ash-coloured, fissured bark; familiar in Japanese woodland; good autumn colour on younger trees; prune late winter and mid-summer; prefers sun but tolerant of partial shade; USDA hardiness zones 4 through 8.

Salix babylonica (weeping willow; shidare-yanagi): 12 m (39 ft); USDA hardiness zones 4 through 9; traditionally planted in Japan near bridges; strictly for large gardens.

Sophora japonica (Japanese pagoda tree; enju): 10 to 25 m (32 ft 6 in to 81 ft); USDA hardiness zones 4 through 8; full sun; deep, rich soil, but tolerates poorer conditions; a spreading, round tree; pinnate leaves; creamy flowers in late summer; can be pruned; can be planted in groups; traditionally an auspicious plant.

Sorbus commixta (Japanese rowan; nana-kamado): 10 to 15 m (32 ft 6 in to 49 ft); USDA hardiness zones 5 through 9; tolerates partial shade; rather dislikes root disturbance; slow-growing; autumn colour and berries.

Zelkova serrata (keaki; keyaki): to 20 m (65 ft); USDA hardiness zones 5 through 8; sun but tolerates partial shade; deep, rich but well-drained soil; deep roots; can be transplanted as a fully grown tree; forms a round shape but does not have a tall central trunk; tolerates hard pruning in winter, though this is not necessary except to maintain a good overall shape; attractive autumn colour; older trees develop a peeling bark exposing an orange-tinted inner bark; resistance to Dutch elm disease; also used for bonsai.

Flowering trees

Camellia japonica (common camellia; yabu-tsubaki): 9 x 8 m (29 x 26 ft); USDA hardiness zones 7 through 9; spreading or upright evergreen shrub or tree; sun; red single flowers with golden trumpet-shaped stamens in late winter, early spring; glossy dark green leaves; rich acid soil; for growing on its own or for hedging; widely grown in Japan; *C. j.* var. *hortensis* (tsubaki) includes garden cultivars, which are pruned, often into a tall column; after flowering cut back branches to a healthy bud, keeping in mind the overall shape of the bush; if necessary, hard prune every six years or so to contain size by cutting back side branches to one or two pairs of leaves (the following year's flowers will be sacrificed); protect plant with mulch against drying out during winter; hybrids appreciate partial shade and need protection against cold winds and late frosts; "Shiro Wabisuke" is a round shrub; small, elegant flowers in midwinter, early spring.

Camellia sasanqua (sazanka): 6 x 3 m (19 ft 6 in x 10 ft); USDA hardiness zones 7 through 9; evergreen columnar shrub or tree; rich, deep, acid soil; tolerates shade and pollution; good as a wind-break; single flowers silky and informal; flowers earlier than common camellia, during the winter in Japan, may bloom in late autumn in some climates; prune late winter after flowering; sunny site for good flowers; protect plant against summer drought.

Cercis chinensis (Chinese redbud; hanazuo): 2 to 5 m (6 ft 7 in to 16 ft); USDA hardiness zones 6 through 9; a deciduous, dense shrub; sun; dark pink flowers in spring before leaves; few pests; resents transplanting when older.

Clethra barbinervis (Japanese clethra/Japanese summersweet; ryobu): a large deciduous shrub or small tree eventually reaching 3 to 6m (10 to 20ft) in height; scented white flowers produced on long spikes July to August; good autumn leaf colour; interesting bark; prefers part shade and moist, slightly acidic soil; avoid dryness; USDA hardiness zones 5 to 8 (plant in sheltered locations in zone 5).

Cornus kousa (yamaboshi): 10 m (32 ft 6 in); USDA hardiness zones 5 through 8; a conical, deciduous tree; sun (but young trees dislike strong summer sun) or partial shade; acid soil; vigorous; tolerates drought; flowers surrounded by four handsome pointed creamy-white bracts produced in early summer, followed by red fruit; keep pruning to a minimum; reduce height by stopping central leader; remove overcrowded branches; can be kept to a small size by removing longer branches at their base; prune late autumn.

Cornus officinalis (sanshuyu): a spreading deciduous shrub; clusters of tiny yellow flowers early in spring; mix with pink *Prunus mume*; reduce height for smaller gardens by cutting back the main stems in late winter every 3 years; USDA hardiness zones 5 through 8.

Hamamelis japonica (Japanese witch hazel; mansaku): 5 to 10 m (16 ft 3 in to 32 ft 6 in); USDA hardiness zones 5 through 8; a shapely deciduous tree; sun but tolerates partial shade; appreciates slightly acid soil; delicately scented yellow or orange ribbon-like flowers in late winter; autumn leaf colour; prune late autumn to maintain size by cutting back same year's growth to above a leaf bud; older trees can be reduced in size by pruning after flowering, cutting back long branches by half or to a side branch; *H. mollis* (Chinese witch hazel) is more common in the West; *H. x intermedia* varieties are hybrids of *H. mollis* and *H. japonica*.

Lagerstroemia indica (crape myrtle; saru-suberi): 4 to 5 m (13 to 16 ft 3 in); USDA hardiness zones 7 through 9; frost hardy (some garden varieties thought to be *L.indica* and *L. fauriei* hybrids are only half hardy); sun; deciduous; long whippy branches; flowers in summer; reduce height for smaller gardens by stopping the central leader at the desired height; grown in Japan with reduced number of lateral branches in order to show off the trunk; prune back laterals late winter or early summer, flower buds will form on the new year's growth.

Magnolia figo (syn. *Michelia figo*; banana shrub/ port-wine magnolia; karatane-ogatama): an evergreen, branching magnolia originating in

facing page, from top left:
Corylopsis spicata
Stewartia pseudocamellia
Single-flowered Kerria japonica
Japanese snowbell (Styrax japonicus)

China; leathery leaves; creamy-white or purple flowers with a scent reminiscent of bananas or port wine in late spring to summer; tolerant of acidic and alkaline soils; regular watering important; full sun for a denser, more compact plant; can be clipped into a hedge; prune after flowering; slow-growing; USDA hardiness zones 8 through 10; frost hardy.

Magnolia kobus (kobushi): 10 to 15 m (32 ft 6 in to 49 ft); USDA hardiness zones 5 through 8; fragrant white flowers in spring before leaves; dislikes root disturbance; tolerant of partial shade and moist, alkaline soil; fragrant leaves; *M. kobus* and *M. liliiflora* will grow tall; stop top growth when desired height is reached; placing a rock under the roots of the tree will encourage roots and branches to spread.

Magnolia liliiflora (shi-mokuren): deciduous; reddish-purple goblet flowers; "Nigra" is shorter (to 2.5 m (8 ft)) with purple-red flowers.

Magnolia obovata (syn. *M. hypoleuca*; Japanese white-bark magnolia/Japanese big-leaf magnolia; ho-no-ki): 20 to 30 m (65 to 97 ft); USDA hardiness zones 5 through 8; fragrant yellow flowers 20 cm (8 in) in diameter, with prominent stamens in spring; fragrant leaves; deciduous.

Magnolia salicifolia (Japanese willow-leaved magnolia; tamu-shiba): USDA hardiness zones 4 through 8; white blossoms in early spring; deciduous leaves have an aniseed scent when crushed; moist, acid conditions; sun or partial shade; closely related to *M. kobus*.

Magnolia sieboldii (oyama-renge): 4 to 5 m (13 to 16 ft 3 in); USDA hardiness zones 6 through 9; creamy, slightly nodding flowers with prominent purplish-red anthers and a fruity scent in late spring, early summer; used for flower arrangements at tea ceremonies; tolerant of moist, alkaline soil; deciduous.

Magnolia stellata (star magnolia; shide-kobushi): 4 to 5 m (13 to 16 ft 3 in); USDA hardiness zones 5 through 8; grows fast in full sun; white fragrant flowers with twelve to eighteen ribbon-like petals in early spring before leaves; rich deep soil; tolerant of alkaline conditions; deciduous.

Magnolia x wieseneri (*M. hypoleuca* x *M. sieboldii*): 6 x 5 m (19 ft 6 in x 16 ft 3 in); USDA hardiness zone 5; heavily scented pendulous white flowers with bright red anthers; deciduous.

Malus halliana (Hall crab apple; hana-kaido): height to 4m (13ft); flowers in May; used also for bonsai; prune in late autumn or late winter, cutting back long branches to within four to six leaf buds; USDA hardiness zones 4 through 8.

Prunus cerasoides var. *rubra* (kanbi-zakura/hi-kanzakura): nodding flowers in late winter before leaves; flowers can be white to deep pink in colour; USDA hardiness zones 7 through 10; half hardy in UK.

Prunus incisa (Fuji cherry; mame-zakura/fuji-zakura): a small wild cherry growing about 3 m (9 ft 9 in) tall; USDA hardiness zones 5 through 7; single, white to pale pink flowers in early spring.

Prunus jamasakura (syn. *Prunus serrulata* var. *spontanea*; Japanese hill cherry; yama-zakura): a wild cherry to 6 m (19 ft 6 in) tall; USDA hardiness zones 4 through 8; young leaves are bronze-coloured; small, pinkish-white flowers; much admired in Japan over the centuries; a parent of hybrid Japanese cherries.

Prunus japonica (oriental bush cherry; niwa-ume): flowers produced in May and edible fruit ripens July to September; moist well-drained soil in full sun or semi-shade; grows to 1.5m (5ft) by 1.5m (5ft); USDA hardiness zones 4 through 8; sometimes referred to as the Japanese bush cherry, but this term is also used for *Prunus maximowiczii* (miyama-zakura).

Prunus mume (Japanese plum/Japanese apricot; ume): 2 to 10 m (6 ft 7 in to 32 ft 6 in); USDA hardiness zones 6 through 8; rich but sandy soil; sun; delicately scented flowers with five white round petals produced in early spring before cherries; yellow fruit in summer; there are cultivars with double flowers, also in shades of pink; reduce branches with flower buds by a third and prune back long spurs with no buds in winter, after the round flower-buds appear; one of the most important flowering trees in Japan; green fruit used for pickles and cordials; "Pendula" (to 6 m (19ft 6 in) tall) is a weeping form with pink flowers.

Prunus sargentii (Sargent cherry; o-yamazakura): a moderate-growing cherry with single pink flowers late April to early May; red leaves and attractive bark; to 10m (32ft) in height; USDA hardiness zones 5 through 8.

Prunus speciosa (Oshima cherry; oshima-zakura) parent of many garden cultivars which are generally referred to in Japanese as *sato-zakura*; famous *sato-zakura* cultivars include "Kanzan/Kwanzan/Sekiyama" (deep double pink flowers before and as the leaves emerge), "Shiro-Fugen" (double white flowers turning pink) and "Taihaku" (large single white); USDA hardiness zones 5 through 9; prone to infection after pruning; choose small or dwarf varieties if space is limited.

Prunus x subhirtella "Pendula" (shidare-zakura): pale flowers emerge before leaves on drooping branches in late winter to early spring; can grow up to 6 to 9m (20 to 30ft) in height, spreading 4.5 to 7.5m (15 to 25ft); USDA hardiness zones 5 through 8; "Autumnalis" (edo-higan-zakura) produces semi-double pale pink flowers intermittently from autumn to spring, other cultivars of this type include "Autumnalis Rosea" and "Jugatsu-zakura".

Prunus x yedoensis (yoshino cherry; somei-yoshino); USDA hardiness zones 6 through 8, warmer areas of zone 5; spreading, arching growth; a weeping form is available.

Stewartia pseudocamellia (natsu-tsubaki/shara-no-ki): up to 10 m (32 ft 6 in); USDA hardiness zones 5 to 8; columnar; rich neutral to acid soil; avoid root disturbance; sun, but hates dry conditions; prune when dormant, only cutting back long side branches at base in order to maintain a balanced shrub shape; white camellia-like flowers in early summer; autumn leaf colour and mottled bark; deciduous; shelter against winter winds; *S. monadelpha* (hime-shara) is smaller.

Styrax japonicus (Japanese snowbell; ego-no-ki): 7 to 8 m (23 to 26 ft); USDA hardiness zones 6 and warmer parts of 5; deciduous; sun but tolerates partial shade; rich, slightly acid soil; water well while settling in; white pendulous flowers like snowdrops in early summer; berries poisonous; prune late winter to maintain shape; for smaller gardens, stop central leader to encourage growth of lateral branches; good autumn colour.

Styrax obassia (fragrant snowbell; haku'unboku): an upright, slender, deciduous tree growing to 6m (20ft); scented bell-like white flowers in late spring; handsome bark on older trees; sun or partial shade; acidic, well-drained but moist soil; prune late winter; USDA hardiness zones 5 through 8, but best planted in protected areas in zone 5.

Shrubs

Evergreen shrubs

Ardisia japonica (marlberry; yabu-koji): 10 to 15 cm (4 to 6 in); USDA hardiness zones 6 through 10; frost hardy in the UK; shady, moist, well-drained conditions; small, leathery leaves and red berries; prune close to the ground in early spring; use for underplanting.

Aucuba japonica (spotted laurel; aoki): 1 to 2 m (3 ft 3 in to 6 ft 7 in); USDA hardiness zones 7 through 10, but may survive colder temperatures if sheltered; rich, moist soil in shade; a round shrub; avoid pruning except to remove old branches at ground level; tolerates pollution; suitable for north-facing gardens, tea gardens, for underplanting; red berries on female plants during winter.

Camellia sinensis (tea; cha-no-ki): an evergreen shrub which can be used for hedges in milder climates; scented white flowers in the autumn; rich, acidic well-drained soil in sun or partial shade; even moisture necessary; prune early spring; USDA hardiness zones 7 through 9.

Elaeagnus x ebbingei (Ebbinge's silverberry/oleaster; gumi): a dense, rounded shrub; leathery

facing page, from top left:
Balloon flower (Platycodon grandiflorus)
Begonia grandis ssp. evansiana *in October*
Chinese lantern (Physalis alkekengi) *in the autumn*
Liriope muscari in October

green leaves; small fragrant flowers in the autumn, followed by small edible fruit; prune branches back to a leaf bud in late winter; prune hard for thick hedges; full sun to partial shade; moist, but well-drained soil; can grow to 2.5 to 3m (8 to10ft); USDA hardiness zones 7 through 9; attractive cultivars with variegated leaves available; *Elaeagnus multiflora* (goumi/gumi/cherry silverberry; gumi/natsu-gumi) is a deciduous shrub, flowering in the spring, and grown for its fruit; USDA hardiness zones 5 through 9.

Euonymus japonicus (Japanese spindle; masaki): a hedge plant; tolerates hard pruning and shaping; clip two to three times a year, mid-spring to early summer and again mid-autumn; when establishing shape (or rejuvenating an older straggly plant), prune hard late winter; varieties with golden leaves, and variegated leaves available; USDA hardiness zones 7 through 10; frost hardy.

Eurya japonica (hi-sakaki): 5 m (16 ft 3 in); USDA zones 8 to 10; frost hardy; partial or complete shade; dislikes hard pruning so clip regularly, two or three times a year to maintain shape and size, best times being early spring, early summer and early autumn; used as hedging around tea gardens; also broad, pruned hedges; flowers smell rather unpleasant.

Fatsia japonica (yatsude): 2 to 3 m (6 ft 7 in to 9 ft 9 in); USDA hardiness zones 8 through 11; frost hardy, with lower temperatures tolerated if sheltered; moist rich soil; sun or dappled shade, full shade in a sheltered position; prune spring, removing old stems to encourage new growth; shrubs can be induced to produce smaller leaves by leaving two or three leaves at the tip of branches and removing the rest.

Juniperus chinensis var. *procumbens* (hai-byakushin): 75 cm x 2 m (2 ft 6 in x 6 ft 7 in); USDA hardiness zones 4 through 9; sun; dry sandy soil especially if alkaline; no pruning; dislikes root disturbance; "Nana" grows to 30 cm (1 ft) tall.

Mahonia japonica (hiiragi-nanten): 1.5 to 2 m (5 ft to 6 ft 7 in); USDA hardiness zones 5 through 9; partial or complete shade; best in acid soils; shorten upright stems to desired height by cutting back to next side branch in late spring, remove old stems at ground level; fragrant yellow flowers in midwinter.

Photinia glabra (red-leaf photinia/Chinese hawthorn; kaname-mochi): vibrant red shoots; clip late spring and then again in late summer; regular clipping recommended as hard pruning can lead to die-back; avoid excessive wet; height to 3 to 5m (10 to 15ft); USDA hardiness zones 8 through 9; frost hardy; *Photinia x fraseri* is a good alternative, tolerating harder pruning; best in full sun and well-drained soil; dislikes being transplanted; USDA hardiness zones 7 through 9; frost hardy.

Pieris japonica (Japanese andromeda; asebi): 2 to 5

m (6 ft 7 in to 16 ft 3 in); USDA hardiness zones 4 through 8; rich, acid soil; partial shade; protect from winter winds; a round bush; white flowers in late winter and spring; light pruning to maintain shrub shape immediately after flowering, remove suckering branches; leaves poisonous if eaten.

Viburnum odoratissimum (sweet viburnum; sangoju): glossy, somewhat coarse, leathery leaves; scented white flowers in late spring and red berries in the autumn; tolerant of pollution and salt air; well-drained but moist soil; traditionally planted in Japan to create a tall screen around the north and western sides of residences; can reach 6m (20 ft) in height; prune late winter; USDA hardiness zones 8 through 10; frost hardy.

Viburnum suspensum (sandanqua viburnum; gomoju): a dense shrub with glossy, coarse, dark green leaves; good for hedges; prune spring through summer to maintain shape and size; crushed leaves emit an odour traditionally likened in Japan to that of roasted sesame seeds but many people find it unpleasant, so trim plants regularly by hand rather than using a hedge trimmer; can grow to 1.8 to 1.3m (6 to 12ft) in height, spreading 1.8m to 3m (6 to 10ft); small, tubular flowers late winter; USDA hardiness zones 8 through 10; frost hardy.

Deciduous shrubs

Berberis thunbergii (Japanese barberry; megi): a thorny, dense, rounded shrub useful for hedges; good autumn colour; prune two or three times a year to maintain size and shape, mid-spring, late summer and autumn; if a less formal style is desired, thin congested branches late winter; 60cm to 2.5m (2 to 8ft) in height, spreading 1 to 2m (4 to 6ft); USDA hardiness zones 4 though 9; it has become invasive in the eastern United States.

Disanthus cercidifolius (red-bud hazel; maruba-no-ki): a rounded shrub growing 1.8 to 3 m (6 to 10ft) in height; round, heart-shaped leaves turning burgundy, orange and crimson in the autumn; moist, humus-rich, acid soil; sun for best autumn colours but partial shade in areas with scorching summer sun; prune back late winter if necessary to lessen size; USDA hardiness zones 5 through 9.

Euonymus alatus (winged euonymus; nishikigi): a dense shrub producing flaming autumn leaf colour; used extensively in gardens in Japan, but has become invasive in the United States.

Euonymus oxyphyllus (Korean spindle tree; tsuribana) a slow-growing, upright tree which can eventually reach 2.5m (8ft) in height; delicate small white flowers in spring; gaudy seed heads ripen in autumn; minimum pruning required; remove over-long branches when the plant is dormant; USDA hardiness zones 4 through 8.

Ilex serrata (Japanese winterberry; ume-modoki): 3 m (9 ft 9 in); USDA hardiness zones 5

through 9; sun; slow-growing but bushy with purple stems; female trees produce red berries, appreciated by birds in winter; bright pink flowers in spring; pruning not necessary except to reduce long spurs.

Lindera umbellata (kuromoji): an elegant shrub which can grow to 3m (9ft) in height; cut back main leaders to desired height late winter; take out old and redundant stems at base to avoid over-crowding; tolerates hard pruning once established; clusters of yellow flowers early spring; moist, acid soil; useful for courtyard gardens in shade; USDA hardiness zones 6 through 9; *Lindera obtusiloba* (danko-bai), which produces vivid yellow flowers (USDA hardiness zones 5 through 9); *Lindera praecox* (abura-chan) (USDA hardiness zones 8 through 11); and *Lindera triloba* (shiromoji) (USDA hardiness zones 7 through 9) are also grown in Japanese gardens.

Salix gracilistyla (rosegold pussy willow; neko-yanagi): 50 cm to 3 m (1 ft 8 in to 9ft 9 in); USDA hardiness zones 5 through 9; a waterside willow with male and female plants; fluffy grey catkins.

Flowering shrubs

Corylopsis pauciflora (buttercup witch hazel; hyuga-mizuki): 1.5 x 2.5 m (5 x 8 ft); USDA hardiness zones 6 through 8; acid soil in sun or partial shade; racemes of pale yellow flowers in spring; deciduous.

Corylopsis spicata (tosa-mizuki): a deciduous shrub of the witch hazel family; lemon-yellow flowers borne in slender, pendant racemes March and April; best pruned immediately after flowering, pruning back long branches to five or six leaves on young plants to encourage flower buds; prune hard for smaller gardens, reducing the number of main stems to two or three; best in acidic, humus-rich, well-drained soil; appreciates partial shade in the afternoon and protection from high winds; height to 1 to 2.5m (4 to 8ft), spreading 2 to 3m (6 to 10ft); USDA hardiness zones 5 through 8.

Daphne odora (jinchoge): 1.5 m (5 ft); reliably winter hardy to USDA zone 7; frost hardy; evergreen; moist, light, acid soil; sun or partial shade; dislikes root disturbance; often pruned to a sphere; cut back branches immediately after flowering; dislikes dry conditions and poor drainage; "Aureomarginata" is more hardy.

Deutzia gracilis (Japanese snow flower; hime-utsugi): USDA hardiness zones 5 through 8; smaller than *D. crenata*; bushy and upright to 1 m

facing page, from top left:
Double day lily (Hemerocallis fulva) *in July.*
White water lily (Nymphaea alba)
Sacred lotus (Nelumbo nucifera)
Lizard's tail (Saururus chinensis)

(3 ft 3 in); white flowers in late spring, early summer; good by waterside.

Enkianthus perulatus (white enkianthus; dodan-tsutsuji): a deciduous shrub which can be used for hedging; heather-like flowers in early spring and flaming red autumn leaf colour; prune immediately after flowering, if desired, always cutting back to the base of a branch or shoot; can be clipped round, also as a tall square hedge; even moisture important for healthy flower buds; height to 30 to 60cm (1 to 2ft); USDA hardiness zones 6 through 8; *E. campanulatus* (red-veined enkianthus; sarasa-dodan), grown for its red-streaked flowers, and *E. cernuus* (nodding enkianthus; shiro-dodan), for its greenish-white blooms, dislike hard pruning and are not suitable for hedges; keep pruning to a minimum by removing congested branches at their base after flowering; rich, neutral to acidic soil for all three species.

Exochorda racemosa (common pearlbush; rikyubai): a deciduous shrub native to China, producing delicate, scented, white flowers late April to May; Japanese name after the great sixteenth-century tea master Sen-no-Rikyu; prefers well-drained, slightly acid soils, but tolerates alkaline; height to 4.5m (15ft), but can be kept compact (1 to 2m, or 3 to 6ft); prune late winter, cutting back long branches to within 10cm (4in) and removing four- to five-year-old branches at their base; USDA hardiness zones 5 through 8.

Gardenia augusta "Radicans"(creeping gardenia; hime-kuchinashi): a dwarf gardenia forming a loose mound approx 30 to 60cm (1 to 2ft) in height, with waxy, heavily scented white flowers early summer; often seen in Japan clipped semi-spherically or into a globe or a dome; can tolerate hard clipping when the shrub is being initially shaped, but flower buds for the following summer will be lost; thereafter trim lightly immediately after flowering in order to maintain shrub size; humus-rich, acidic, evenly moist but well-drained soil; appreciates partial shade in the afternoons during the summer; protect from cold winds during winter; USDA hardiness zones 8 through 10; frost tender in the UK (minimum temperature 10°C/50°F).

Hibiscus mutabilis (Confederate rose mallow; fuyo): prune stems to the desired height in early spring; USDA hardiness zones 7 through 10; frost tender in the UK (minimum temperature 13°C/55°F); *H. syriacus* (mukuge) is tolerant of hard pruning if size control is necessary; prune late winter; thin out congested stems; hardy down to -15°C/5°F.

Hypericum patulum (kinshibai): evergreen or semi-evergreen rounded shrub of the St. John's wort family, introduced to Japan from China in the middle of the eighteenth century; yellow cup-shaped flowers from August to October; trim lightly after flowering, rejuvenate every four or five years by cutting all stems to 20cm (8in) above ground level; USDA hardiness zones 6 through 7; a very handsome alternative is *Hypericum* x *inordorum* reaching approx. 1m (3ft) in height; recommended cultivars include "Ysella", "Rheingold" and "Summer Gold"; small single yellow flowers appear on same year's growth; yellow-green leaves; striking red berries produced in the summer; prune hard at the end of winter; suitable for smaller gardens; best in semi-shade; USDA hardiness zones 7 through 9.

Hydrangea macrophylla (lacecap and hortensia hydrangeas; ajisai): 1.5 to 2 m (5 to 6 ft 7 in); USDA hardiness zones 5 through 9; moist rich soil; acid soil with a pH reading of less than 5.5 will produce blue flowers, a pH reading greater than 5.5 will produce pink flowers; white-flowering varieties not affected; tolerates shade; prune back flowering branches to the next non-flowering branch immediately after flowering; will cease to flower well on older stems; renew every three to four years by cutting back stems to two or three nodes above ground level after flowering; useful in north-facing gardens or for interplanting between trees.

Hydrangea paniculata (nori-utsugi): 3 m (9 ft 9 in); USDA hardiness zones 4 through 7; partial shade; fast-growing; takes pruning; for underplanting.

Hydrangea quercifolia (oak-leaf hydrangea; kashiwa-ajisai): white- to cream-coloured flowers produced in large panicles June-July; hot summers for best blooms; single blossom types and doubles available; large coarse leaves resembling oak leaves, producing good autumn colour; good drainage essential; prune branches which have flowered to desired length, aiming for an overall semi-spherical shrub shape; can reach 2m (6ft) in height; native to south-eastern North America and popular in Japan; USDA hardiness zones 6 through 9.

Kerria japonica (yamabuki): 2 x 2.5 m (6 ft 6 in x 8 ft); USDA hardiness zones 4 through 9; moist, rich soil; sun or partial shade; yellow single or double flowers in spring; pruning not required unless the plant is too big; prune early spring by cutting back over-long branches; thin out non-flowering and older branches at base; rejuvenate every four or five years by cutting back the entire shrub to within 20 cm (8in) after flowering.

Lespedeza bicolor (Japanese bush clover; yama-hagi): 1.5 to 2 m (5 to 6 ft 7 in); USDA hardiness zones 5 through 8; sun; good in groups; rich soil; tiny purple-pink flowers at the end of summer and in autumn; weeping branches; prune if necessary after leaf-fall; cut back old branches to the ground and reduce younger branches by half; *L. thunbergii*: a subshrub; cut back branches to within 10 cm (4 in) of the ground; cv. "Albiflora" has white flowers; cv. "Versicolor" has white and rosy purple flowers on the same plant.

Loropetalum chinense (Chinese fringe flower; tokiwa-mansaku): an evergreen shrub of the witch hazel family producing scented, white flowers late winter or early spring; "Rubrum" and other cultivars have pink or red flowers with bronze-red early foliage; new foliage appears late summer to autumn; prune back over-long shoots immediately after flowering to maintain shrub shape and size; suitable also for containers; prefers humus-rich, acidic, moist, well-drained soil; do not allow to get dry; best full sun with partial shade in the afternoons; USDA hardiness zones 7 through 10; frost-hardy to half-hardy in the UK.

Osmanthus fragrans f. *aurantiacus* (fragrant olive/sweet tea; kin-mokusei): to 10 m (32 ft 6 in); USDA hardiness zones 8 through 10; half hardy; clusters of tiny orange blooms with an intense fruity scent in autumn; prune into a column; when growing from a sapling, stop top growth; cut back long branches in winter to prune into the desired shape; allow it to become slightly bigger each year to encourage buds on new growth.

Paeonia suffruticosa (tree peony/moutan; botan): to 2 m (6 ft 7 in); USDA hardiness zones 4 through 8; a deciduous shrub; sun; shallow roots; resents strong afternoon sunlight and dry conditions; humus-rich soil; resents root disturbance; many cultivars; prune down to one or two flowering buds in late autumn.

Philadelphus satsumi (baika-utsugi): deciduous, upright shrub of the mock-orange family with showy, scented flowers in summer; remove older stems at base in late autumn or early spring; height to 2 to 2.5m (6 to 8ft); USDA hardiness zone 7; frost hardy.

Rhaphiolepis umbellata (Yeddo hawthorn/Indian hawthorn; sharinbai): an evergreen shrub native to Japan and Korea, with small, oval, leathery leaves and clusters of star-like, white flowers in early summer; tolerates heavy pruning if necessary (but avoid cutting back to leafless old wood); lightly clip to maintain shape immediately after flowering; remove suckering branches; flowers best in full sun; good for hedges; height to 5ft (1.5m); USDA hardiness zones 8 through 10, warmer areas of zone 7; frost hardy.

[*Rhododendron*] *Satsuki-tsutsuji* (satsuki for short) is the name by which *Rhododendron indicum* and its garden cultivars are known in Japan; they are small-leaved, dense, evergreen azaleas, growing 30cm to 90cm (1 to 3ft) in height, with bright pink funnel-shaped flowers in late May; tolerant of hard pruning, they are invariably clipped in Japan, and since the seventeenth century have become an essential part of all types of Japanese gardens,

right: Phyllostachys edulis *underplanted with hortensia (mophead) hydrangeas* (Hydrangea macrophylla)

being used as single specimens, or as rounded hedges or square hedges; frequently several large plants are grown and clipped together to form a single large bush; acidic, well-drained but moisture-retentive soil; trim into shape while the last flowers are still on the plant; can be pruned hard to reduce size, but next year's flowers will be sacrificed; USDA hardiness zones 7 through 8.

[*Rhododendron*]*Shakunage* refers to evergreen rhododendrons with big leathery leaves; native Japanese species include *R. yakushimanum* (hosoha-shakunage); to 4 m (13 ft) in height; rich, well-drained, acid soil in half-shade; slow-growing; they dislike pruning and root disturbance.

[*Rhododendron*]*Tsutsuji*: Tsutsuji is the Japanese term covering all azaleas, both evergreen and deciduous; evergreen and semi-evergreen azaleas include *R. kaempferi* (yama-tsutsuji), *R. kiusianum* (miyama-kirishima), *R. x obtusum* (kirishima-tsutsuji) and *R. pulchrum* (o-murasaki-tsutsuji), as well as Hirado hybrids, the dwarf Kurume hybrids and *R. indicum* (satsuki-tsutsuji) hybrids; vigorous and suitable for hard pruning; excellent for group planting and broad, pruned hedges; prune when the last flowers are still on the bush; to reduce the size of a plant that has become too large, cut back half the branches to a size smaller than the desired one; the following year prune back the rest of the branches.

R. quinquefolium (shiro-yashio/goyo-tsutsuji), *R. dilatatum* (mitsuba-tsutsuji), *R. reticulatum* (koba-no-mitsuba-tsutsuji) and *R. japonicum* (renge-tsutsuji): deciduous azaleas; not vigorous; should be tidied only if necessary to remove weak, dead or crossed branches immediately after flowering; *R. quinquefolium* is a delicate small tree; white flowers with green speckles among leaves produced in whorls of five; USDA hardiness zones 6 through 8, but protect it.

Serissa foetida (syn. *Serissa japonica*; snowrose/tree-of-a-thousand-stars/serissa; hakuchoge): a semi-evergreen shrub to 60 to 120cm (2 to 4ft) in height; white flowers produced late spring to early summer; can drop up to half of its leaves in the winter while still young; used for bonsai but also traditionally as a pruned hedging plant in warmer areas of Japan; varieties with variegated leaves available; prune after flowering, lightly clip again in autumn if necessary to maintain shape and size; older plants can be rejuvenated with hard pruning in April; short-lived (about ten years); easily propagated by taking either softwood cuttings in the spring or ripewood cuttings in the summer; bruised leaves have an unpleasant smell; USDA hardiness zones 7 through 11, depending on individual cultivars; frost tender in the UK (minimum temperature 7 ° C/45 ° F).

Spiraea cantoniensis (Reeves's spiraea; kodemari): 1 to 2 m (3 ft 3 in to 6 ft 7 in); USDA hardiness zones 7 through 9, may survive in zones 5 and 6 if planted in a protected location; a deciduous or semi-evergreen shrub; flowers mid-spring; rich soil; sun; fast-growing; can be pruned into a sphere; prune after flowering, cutting back to an upward-turning bud; every three years cut back old branches to fresh young growth at the base of the plant.

Spiraea japonica (shimotsuke): a clump-forming, deciduous shrub, growing to 1.2 to 1.8m (4 to 6ft) in height but usually around 80cm (30in); flowers May through to July; dead-head for continuous flowering; cut back to 30cm (12in) above ground level after flowering every three to five years to rejuvenate plant; full sun; autumn leaf colour; USDA hardiness zones 3 through 8.

Spiraea thunbergii (baby's breath spirea/breath-of-spring spirea; yuki-yanagi): 1 to 1.5 m (3 ft 3 in to 5 ft); USDA hardiness zones 4 through 8; flowers in early spring; sun: trailing branches; remove congested stems at base; rejuvenate older shrubs by cutting back the entire plant to within 30cm (12in); prune immediately after flowering; deciduous.

Stachyurus praecox (kibushi): a deciduous shrub growing to 1 to 1.5m (3 to 5ft) in height, with a wide, upright vase shape and strong growth; striking racemes of yellow flowers resembling a bead curtain in March; good autumn leaf colour; remove older flowering stems after three years to avoid overcrowding; full sun to partial shade; well-drained, acidic to neutral soil; USDA hardiness zones 7 through 8.

Viburnum furcatum (forked viburnum/scarlet-leaved viburnum; mushikari): a deciduous shrub to 3.5m (11 ½ft) in height; scented, white flowers resembling lacecap hydrangeas produced in May; veined leaves, good autumn colour; berries in October but not-self-fertile; moist acid to neutral soil; tolerant of semi-shade; USDA hardiness zones 5 through 9.

Viburnum japonicum (hakusanboku): to 1.8 m (6 ft); USDA hardiness zones 7 through 9; round, evergreen shrub; small, fragrant, white flowers in round cymes in early summer; sun; grows fast; takes hard pruning.

Viburnum phlebotrichum (otoko-yozome): to 2.5m (8ft); small, white flowers but plants are not self-fertile; leaves turn crimson in the autumn; deciduous; USDA hardiness zone 5.

Viburnum plicatum (Japanese snowball; odemari): to 3 m (9 ft 9 in); USDA hardiness zones 5 through 8; a deciduous shrub producing large, spherical, white flowerheads; other cultivars, which have lacecape flowers, are sometimes described as *V. plicatum* f. *tomentosum*; sun; slow growth; light pruning; good as a specimen plant for a front garden.

Berries

Ardisia crenata (coralberry; manryo): 60 cm to 1 m (2 ft to 3 ft 3 in); evergreen; berries from winter to spring below leaves growing from the top of the plant; cut back stem every four or five years in spring to reduce height; dappled shade to full shade; USDA hardiness zones 8 through 10; half hardy; has become invasive in Florida, southern Africa and parts of the east coast of Australia.

Ardisia crispa (spiceberry; kara-tachibana/hyaku-ryo): a small evergreen shrub with narrow, glossy, dark green leaves and colourful clusters of red berries (toxic) in late autumn; shade tolerant; 20 to 80cm (8 to 30in) in height; varieties with red or yellow berries also available; USDA hardiness zones 8 through 9; half hardy.

Callicarpa japonica (Japanese beauty-berry; murasaki-shikibu): 3 to 5 m (9 ft 9 in to 16 ft 3 in); USDA hardiness zones 5 through 8; sun; deciduous; can be pruned close to the ground in the late autumn or early spring, but do not prune the tips of branches; stems die back to the ground in cold areas; purple berries in autumn; for informal shrubbery; named after Murasaki Shikibu, author of *The Tale of Genji*; *C. dichotoma* (ko-murasaki) is smaller.

Sarcandra glabra (senryo): 60 cm to 90 cm (2 to 3 ft); USDA hardiness zones 8 and 9; half hardy, but shelter in winter and mulch; evergreen; grown for red winter berries; partial shade; use for under-planting; do not let leaves burn in hot sun; fast growth; tolerant of sea air; hates dry conditions; if a bigger plant is desired, reduce branches to a leaf node in late winter; often grown with *Ardisia crenata* (manryo).

Nandina domestica (heavenly bamboo; nanten): 1.5 to 2 m (5 ft to 6 ft 7 in), but some cultivars are shorter; USDA hardiness zones 5 through 10; sun or partial shade; evergreen or semi-evergreen; red berries in winter months; dark purple-green leaves; planted under eaves of houses – not, as E. A. Bowles (1865–1954), the English horticulturalist, suggested, because the wood was used as tooth-picks, but to prevent the flowers being splashed by rain; replant in autumn and mulch; remove old and dead branches in early spring, and cut back tips of stems for branching shape; an auspicious plant.

Ground-cover

Epimedium grandiflorum var. *thunbergianum* (bishop's hat; ikari-so): a clump-forming, herbaceous perennial with flowers ranging in colour from pink, yellow, white through to purple; a good, non-invasive ground-cover plant; cut back foliage late winter; divide clumps early spring or autumn; rich, well-drained acid soil; full shade or partial shade;

facing page, from top left:
Toad lily (Tricyrtis hirta)
Enkianthus perulatus
Kirishima azalea (Rhododendron x obtusum)
at the Isui-en garden in Nara, Japan
Japanese beauty-berry (Callicarpa dichotoma)

height to 45cm (18in), spreading 15 to 45cm (6 to 18in); USDA hardiness zones 5 through 8 (deciduous in zones 5 through 6).

Ophiopogon japonicus (Japanese snake's beard/ mondo grass; ryu-no-hige/ja-no-hige): 10 to 30 cm (4 to 12 in); USDA hardiness zones 7 through 10; prefers moist, slightly acid conditions and shade; top-dress with leaf mould in autumn; flower-spikes in summer; strap-like narrow leaves 10 to 20 cm (4 to 8 in); forms dense ground-cover; tolerates low light (good under eaves to prevent mud splashing); *O. planiscapus* "Nigrescens" (oba-janohige "Kokuryu") has black leaves, lilac flowers, followed by blue berries, and is hardy; *O. jaburan* (no-shiran) has striped variegated forms, and is hardy.

Reineckea carnea (kichijo-so): 8 to 13 cm (3 ¼ to 7 ¼ in) tall; USDA hardiness zones 7 through 10; neutral to acid soil; partial shade; evergreen; good for ground-cover; blooms in late autumn.

Saxifraga stolonifera (yuki-no-shita): (8 in to 1 ft 8 in); USDA hardiness zones 6 through 9; evergreen perennial, with thick, kidney-shaped leaves, purplish underneath with white veins; white flowers in late spring to early summer; prefers wet, shady, rocky places; requires very little soil.

Syneilesis palmata (shredded umbrella plant; yabure-gasa) a non-invasive, deciduous ground-cover plant; deeply toothed, 15cm (6in)-wide, palmate leaves with jagged edges; umbels of white flowers on stalks June-July; rich, moist soil in partial shade or shade; to 30 cm (12in)in height; USDA hardiness zones 5 through 9.

Grasses and Bamboos

Grasses

Carex hachijoensis "Evergold" (hachijo-kansuge): 30 x 35 cm (1 ft x 1 ft 2 in); USDA hardiness zones 5 through 10; a creamy yellow and green, variegated variety of a tufted, evergreen sedge; moist well-drained conditions in sun or partial shade.

Hakonechloa macra "Aureola" (uraha-gusa/fuchi-so): 36 x 40 cm (1 ft 2 ½ in x 1 ft 4 in); USDA hardiness zones 5 through 9; a variegated form of a deciduous, clump-forming, perennial grass; bright gold with green stripes, red-tinted in the autumn; moist soil, partial shade for good colour.

Imperata cylindrica "Rubra" (Japanese blood-grass; chigaya): *I. cylindrica*, known as cogongrass, is highly invasive; "Rubra" is a horticultural selection which does not set seed and is propagated by division; because US states have different regulations regarding this plant, it is important to check; USDA hardiness zones 5 through 9, but less aggressive in cooler climates; leaves to 50 cm (1 ft 8 in) long, tips turning blood-red.

Miscanthus sinensis (Chinese silvergrass; susuki); *Phragmites australis* (common reed; ashi): both plants, especially the former, have important cultural associations for the Japanese, but they are highly invasive; consider alternatives such as those listed below.

Muhlenbergia capillaris (pink muhlygrass): superb pink flower plumes in the autumn; best in sandy or rocky, well-drained soils in full sun; height to 90cm (3ft), spreading 90cm (3ft); USDA hardiness zones 5 through 9.

Schizachyrium scoparium (little bluestem): height to 1.2m (4ft); cut back old foliage late winter to early spring; USDA hardiness zones 3 through 9.

Sorghastrum nutans (Indian grass): height to 90 to 150cm (3 to 5ft); cut back old foliage late winter to early spring to encourage new growth; USDA hardiness zones 4 through 9.

Sporobolus heterolepis (prarie dropseed): slow-to-establish but long-lived grass native to North America; scented flowers late summer through to early autumn; 60 to 90cm (2 to 3ft) in height; USDA hardiness zones 3 through 9.

Bamboos

Bambusa multiplex (hedge bamboo): 3 to 5 m (9 ft 9 in to 16 ft 3 in); USDA hardiness zones 8 and above; half hardy; shoots appear from summer into autumn; *B. multiplex* and the related *Bambusa textilis* are clump-forming bamboos and are usually not invasive in habit; *B. multiplex* var. *elegans* (ho'o-chiku) has stems grow up to 3m (10ft) and small leaves (variegated cultivars available); *B. multiplex* "Alphonse Karr" (suho-chiku) has spotted leaves and yellow stems streaked green in winter and red in the summer; *B. multiplex* f. *solida* (komachi-dake) has non-hollow culms.

Chimonobambusa marmorea (kan-chiku): up to 3 m (9 ft 9 in); USDA hardiness zones 8 through 10; shade; for hedging; likes a warm climate; rich soil; a bamboo with solid (not hollow) stems and red, mottled culms; can become highly invasive in warm and moist locations; contain roots by establishing a trench and cutting away emerging rhizomes, together with using a specialist plastic root barrier for bamboos.

Hibanobambusa tranquillans (inyo-chiku): 3 to 5 m (9 ft 9 in to 16 ft 3 in); USDA hardiness zones 7 through 9; acid soil; a hardy hybrid of *Sasa* and *Phyllostachys*; large leaves and smooth bamboo-like canes; used for hedges; tolerates drought; can become invasive; contain roots by establishing a trench and cutting away emerging rhizomes, together with using a specialist plastic root barrier for bamboos.

Phyllostachys bambusoides (ma-dake): 10 to 20 m (32 ft 6 in to 65 ft); USDA hardiness zones 7 through 10; sun; rich soil in warmer climates; difficult to transplant; for bamboo groves;

harvested for fencing and crafts; "Castillonis" (kimmei-chiku): 8 to 10 m (26 ft to 32 ft 6 in); hardy; golden-yellow culms and green leaves marked creamy-white or yellow; has the potential to become invasive; contain roots by establishing a trench and cutting away emerging rhizomes, together with using a specialist plastic root barrier for bamboos.

Phyllostachys edulis (moso-dake): 15 to 20 m (49 to 65 ft); USDA hardiness zones 8 through 10; the thickest bamboo; used for bamboo groves; shoots eaten; prune spring; cut off top at desired height and remove congested branches, shortening long branches to desired length and removing old culms; has the potential to become invasive; contain roots by establishing a trench and cutting away emerging rhizomes, together with using a specialist plastic root barrier for bamboos.

Phyllostachys nigra (kuro-chiku): 2 to 3 m (6 ft 7 in to 9 ft 9 in); USDA hardiness zones 7 and above, but dies back in winter in cold areas; canes are dark green the first year, turning black from the second; shade; for a small courtyard garden or as background; has the potential to become invasive; contain roots by establishing a trench and cutting away emerging rhizomes, together with using a specialist plastic root barrier for bamboos.

Phyllostachys pubescens var. *heterocycla* (syn. *P. heterocycla* f. *pubescens*; kikko-chiku): USDA hardiness zones 7 and above; a *P. edulis* mutation; joints zig-zag up the culms which bulge between the joints; an unusual and rare ornamental bamboo.

Phyllostachys sulphurea (ogon-ko-chiku): to 8 m (26 ft); USDA hardiness zones 7 and above; green canes turn bright yellow streaked with green; can become invasive; contain roots by establishing a trench and cutting away emerging rhizomes, together with using a specialist plastic root barrier for bamboos.

Pleioblastus simonii (me-dake): to 6m (10ft) in height; USDA hardiness zones 7 through 10; a good hedging bamboo, but highly invasive; contain roots by establishing a trench and cutting away emerging rhizomes, together with using a specialist plastic root barrier for bamboos, otherwise cultivate in a container.

Semiarundinaria fastuosa (temple bamboo/ Narihira bamboo; narihira-dake): a tall, upright, hardy bamboo with green culms striped burgundy-brown when young, which can become flushed purple in a sunny location; to 7m (25ft) in height; prune spring; cut top at desired height and remove

facing page, from top left:

Iris ensata

Iris laevigata *growing alongside a* yatsuhashi *bridge in the Koishikawa Koraku-en garden, Tokyo*

Iris japonica, *also known as the fringed iris*

congested branches, shortening long branches to desired length; old culms will lose their colour and should be removed; USDA hardiness zones 7 through 10; warmer areas of zone 6; potential to become invasive; contain roots by establishing a trench and cutting away emerging rhizomes; use specialist roor barrier.

Semiarundinaria kagamiana (rikuchu-dake): 3 to 5 m (9 ft 9 in to 16 ft 3 in); USDA hardiness zones 6 through 9; bushy; tolerates both sun and shade; can become very invasive; contain roots by establishing a trench and cutting away emerging rhizomes, together with using a specialist plastic root barrier for bamboos.

Semiarundinaria yashadake "Kimmei": USDA hardiness zones 7 through 10; yellow culms tinted pink and green, turning dusky red in sunlight during their first winter; has the potential to become very invasive; contain roots by establishing a trench and cutting away emerging rhizomes, together with using a specialist plastic root barrier for bamboos.

Sinobambusa tootsik (to-chiku): recommended for USDA hardiness zones 9 and 10; hardy down to -10°C/14°F; usually pruned; stop top when 3 to 8 m (9 ft 9 in to 26 ft) in height; side shoots selected for rounded leaf growth, all other side shoots removed; can become very invasive; contain roots by establishing a trench and cutting away emerging rhizomes, together with using a specialist plastic root barrier for bamboos.

Tetragonocalamus quadrangularis (shiho-chiku): 5 to 6 m (16 ft 3 in to 19 ft 6 in); canes flattened on all four sides; shoots produced in the autumn and winter; shade; rich soil; difficult to transplant; good for small courtyard gardens; USDA hardiness zones 8 through 11; frost hardy; can become highly invasive; contain roots by establishing a trench and cutting away emerging rhizomes, together with using a specialist plastic root barrier for bamboos.

Shorter bamboo grasses

Prune dwarf bamboos and sasas by cutting back the plants to their desired size. This is best done in early spring before new bamboo shoots emerge from the ground.

Pleioblastus auricoma (kamuro-zasa): 30 cm to 1.5 m (1 ft to 5 ft); USDA hardiness zones 8 through 10; gold and green variegated leaves; likes shade; can become very invasive; contain roots by establishing a trench and cutting away emerging rhizomes, together with using a specialist plastic root barrier for bamboos.

Pleioblastus variegatus (chigo-zasa); 30 cm to 1 m (1 ft to 3 ft 3 in); USDA hardiness zones 7 through 10; makes a thick and bushy clump; green and cream variegated leaves; can become very invasive; contain roots by establishing a trench and

cutting away emerging rhizomes, together with using a specialist plastic root barrier for bamboos.

Sasa palmata (broad-leaf bamboo; chimaki-zasa): a ground-cover bamboo but extremely invasive; contain roots by establishing a trench and cutting away emerging rhizomes, together with using a specialist plastic root barrier for bamboos.

Sasa tsuboïana (ibuki-zasa): 1.5 to 2 m (5 ft to 6 ft 7 in); USDA hardiness zones 7 through 9, warmer areas of zone 6; forms round clumps with dark green leaves; can become highly invasive; contain roots by establishing a trench and cutting away emerging rhizomes, together with using a specialist plastic root barrier for bamboos.

Sasa veitchii (kuma-zasa): to 90 cm (3 ft); USDA hardiness zones 6 through 9; for dense ground-cover; coarse leaves; highly invasive; contain roots by establishing a trench and cutting away emerging rhizomes, together with using a specialist plastic root barrier for bamboos.

Sasamorpha borealis (suzu-take): an upright, cold-hardy bamboo; to 2m (6ft) in height; USDA hardiness zones 6 through 9; can become very invasive; contain roots by establishing a trench and cutting away emerging rhizomes, together with using a specialist plastic root barrier for bamboos.

Sasaella ramosa (azuma-zasa): a good ground-cover bamboo but highly invasive; always contain roots by establishing a trench and cutting away emerging rhizomes, together with using a specialist plastic root barrier for bamboos; height 45 to 90cm (1½-3ft); USDA hardiness zones 7 through 9.

Shibataea kumasaca (okame-zasa): 1 to 2 m (3 ft 3 in to 6 ft 7 in); USDA hardiness zones 6 through 9; shade; for ground-cover or wide, pruned hedges; can become invasive; contain roots by establishing a trench and cutting away emerging rhizomes, together with using a specialist plastic root barrier for bamboos.

Mosses

Mosses used in Japan

Mosses need an acid, moist but well-drained environment. Transplant them early in spring.

Polytrichum formosum (o-sugi-goke), *P. commune* (common haircap moss; uma-sugi-goke), *Pogonatum inflexum* (niwa-sugi-goke), *Racomitrium japonicum* (suna-goke), *Hypnum plumaeforme* (hai-goke), *Rhizogonium dozyanum* (hinoki-goke), *Thuidium tamariscinum* (common tamarisk-moss; o-shinobu-goke), *Campylopus japonicus* (yamato-fude-goke), *Leucobryum neilgherrense* (hosoba-shiraga-goke/yama-goke), *Dicranum scoparium* (broom fork-moss; kamoji-goke).

Alternatives

Arenaria tetraquetra: hardy to zone 7; forms a dense

evergreen mat; star-shaped white flowers in the spring.

Hypnum cupressiforme (hypnum moss): a moss widespread around the world; adaptable to various climate zones and habitats; partial to full shade.

Leucobryum glaucum (cushion moss): USDA hardiness zones 6 through 10.

Thuidium delicatulum (delicate fern moss; koba-no-ezo-shinobu-goke): a moss found in North and South America, the West Indies, Europe and Asia; hardy to warmer areas of USDA hardiness zone 6; moist, acid soil; dappled to full shade.

Selaginella kraussiana (Krauss's spikemoss): USDA hardiness zones 7 through 9; frost tender in the UK (minimum temperature 5-7°C/41-45°F); an evergreen, South African perennial that forms a dense mat; moist to wet, acidic soil.

Ferns

Adiantum aleuticum (Aleutian maidenhair fern; kujaku-shida): 75 x 75 cm (2 ft 6 in x 2 ft 6 in); USDA hardiness zones 3 through 9; deciduous or semi-evergreen; thought to look like the plumes of a peacock tail.

Blechnum nipponicum (shishigashira/iwashi-bone/mukade-gusa): hardy to USDA hardiness zone 7; hardy to at least -10°C/14°F (best protected in colder regions); an evergreen fern; partial or full shade; moist acid soil; upright leathery fronds, likened to a lion's mane, centipedes, or the backbone of a sardine.

Cyrtomium macrophyllum (hiroha-yabu-sotetsu): 45 x 60 cm (1 ft 6 in x 2 ft); USDA hardiness zones 6 through 10; evergreen, large-leaved holly fern; also *C. fortunei* (yabu-sotetsu), USDA hardiness zones 6 through 10; and *C. falcatum* (oni-yabu-sotetsu), semi-evergreen or deciduous in colder places, USDA hardiness zones 6 through 11, needing shelter.

Davallia mariesii (hare's foot fern; shinobu); 15 cm (6 in) in height; perennial in USDA hardiness zones 9 through 11; hardy in the UK; deciduous; finely cut fronds.

Dryopteris erythrosora (Japanese red shield fern/painted fern; beni-shida): USDA hardiness zones 5 through 11; a deciduous fern growing from reddish shoots; *Athyrium niponicum*, USDA hardiness zones 3 through 8, also grows from a red root-stock and has purple-tinted, green fronds; both need moisture in shade; neutral to acid soil; mulch well when planting.

Equisetum hyemale (tokusa): a perennial related to ferns and native to parts of North America,

facing page, from top:

Sago palms (Cycas revoluta) *in a garden*
Magnolia sieboldii

Europe and northern Asia; USDA hardiness zones 3 through 11; grown for upright stalks to 50 cm (1 ft 8 in); good for planting around water basins; can spread aggressively, so use root barriers; invasive in moist habitats in South Africa and Australia.

Matteuccia struthiopteris (ostrich fern/kusa-sotetsu): USDA hardiness zones 3 through 7; deciduous with upright fronds; spreading; neutral to acid soil in open shade.

Polystichum polyblepharum (Japanese tassel fern; inode): 60 to 90 cm (2 to 3 ft); USDA hardiness zones 5 through 8; an evergreen fern with shuttle-cock fronds.

Selaginella tamariscina (iwa-hiba): USDA hardiness zones 8 to 10, warmer areas of zone 7; an evergreen perennial with a long stalk and scaly leaves; grows on rocky terrain; likes moderately rich, moist, well-drained, neutral to slightly acid soil, and partial shade.

Tropical Specimen Plants

Cycas revoluta (Japanese sago palm/Japan fern palm; sotetsu): 3 to 8 m (9 ft 9 in to 26 ft); USDA hardiness zones 9 through 11, warmer areas of zone 8; frost tender (minimum temperature 7-10°C/45-50°F); can survive colder temperatures with protection during winter months; full sun; in early summer when new leaves have emerged, remove the previous year's leaves; in cooler areas, protect the crown with straw against cold; hates wet.

Musa basjoo (Japanese banana; basho): to 5 m (16 ft 3 in) tall; USDA hardiness zones 5 through 10; a perennial with arching leaf blades; neutral to slightly acid, well-drained soil; the haiku poet Matsuo Basho (1644–94) took his name from this plant.

Foliage and Flowers

Foliage

Aspidistra elatior (ha-ran): USDA hardiness zones 8 through 10; frost hardy; perennial with dark, glossy leaves; for tea gardens; shade tolerant.

Farfugium japonicum (tsuwabuki): 30 cm (1 ft); USDA hardiness zones 7 through 10; frost hardy; evergreen; partial or complete shade; glossy leaves; dislikes dry conditions.

Hosta spp. (plantain lily; giboshi): partial or full shade, but yellow-leaved varieties appreciate some sun with midday protection; hates dry conditions; mulch in spring; leaves ovate, lance-shaped, round or heart-shaped; tall spikes of flowers in summer; *H. plantaginea* var. *japonica* (fragrant plantain lily; tama-no-kanzashi) has yellow-green leaves (USDA hardiness zones 3 through 9); *H. sieboldiana* (seersucker plantain lily) has matte blue-green leaves (USDA hardiness zones 3 through 8).

Pachysandra terminalis (Japanese spurge; fukki-so): 25 x 60 cm (10 in x 2 ft); USDA hardiness zones 5 through 8; evergreen ground-cover; prostrate glossy leaves in whorls; white berries; slightly acid to neutral soil, if the latter give plants acid fertilizer yearly; partial or deep shade; pinch out tips for the first two to three years; has become very invasive in several US states; keep confined to maintained gardens and do not plant in woodland or along stream banks.

Rohdea japonica (Japanese sacred lily; omoto): USDA hardiness zones 6 through 10; an evergreen perennial producing leathery leaves up to 30 cm (1 ft) in length; in summer produces greenish-yellow flower-heads followed by red or white berries; moist, acid soil in shade.

Flowers

Arisaema thunbergii subsp. *urashima* (urashima-so): a herbaceous perennial producing a jack-in-the-pulpit-like spathe, green and purple with white stripes; poisonous roots; prefers partial to full shade and humus-rich, moist, well-drained soil; 8 to 10cm (3 to 4in) in height; USDA hardiness zones 5 through 9.

Aster tartaricus (shion): to 2 m (6 ft 7 in); USDA hardiness zones 3 through 7; a pale, delicate lavender aster flowering in autumn; moist soil; dislikes shade; "Jin-Dai" is a more compact cultivar growing to 1m (4ft) in height.

Astilbe (chidake-sashi): dwarf hybrids include "Sprite", which has dark foliage and pale pink flower-spikes in summer, growing to about 30 cm (1 ft) tall; USDA hardiness zones 4 through 8; rich, moist soil in partial shade.

Begonia grandis subsp. *evansiana* (shukaido): to 50 cm (1 ft 8 in); USDA hardiness zones 6 through 9, but protect against winter cold; perennial with fleshy stalks flushed red around the nodes; pale red single flowers from summer into autumn.

Bletilla striata (shi-ran): USDA hardiness zones 5 through 9; a deciduous terrestrial orchid; moist, rich soil; partial shade; lance-shaped leaves; bright pink flowers in spring to early summer; mulch in autumn in colder areas, or lift and store in a dry, frost-free place.

Calanthe discolor (ground orchid; ebine): a woodland orchid from Japan bearing maroon and white flowers on a tall stem in late spring or early summer; partial shade in moist, humus rich, well-drained, acidic to neutral soil (allow it to go dry in the winter); USDA hardiness zones 6 through 9.

Chelonopsis moschata (jako-so): a slow-spreading perennial producing tiny, deep mauve penstamon-like flowers in late summer through to autumn; to 60cm (24in) in height; damp, partial shade; USDA hardiness zones 5 through 9.

Chloranthus japonicus (hitori-shizuka): a dainty perennial producing a single spike of white, scented, bottlebrush-like flowers in the spring; partial shade; moist, well-drained soil; height to 60cm (24in), spreading to 90cm (36in); USDA hardiness zones 6 through 9.

Chloranthus serratus (futari-shizuka): produces two spikes of scented, white, bottlebrush-like flowers; moist, well-drained soil in partial shade; USDA hardiness zones 6 through 9.

Clintonia udensis (tsubame-omoto): 30 x 20 cm (1 ft x 8 in); USDA hardiness zones 5 through 8; a herbaceous, clump-forming perennial; fertile, moist, neutral to acid soil; partial or full shade; bell-shaped white flowers in racemes in summer.

Dicentra peregrina (bleeding-heart; koma-gusa): a Japanese herbaceous perennial of the bleeding-heart family; USDA hardiness zones 5 through 7; Dicentra "King of Hearts", which produces 20cm (8in)-high clusters of red, heart-shaped flowers from spring into early summer, is a cross between two North American dicentras (*D. eximia* and *D. formosa*) and *D. peregrina*; dead-head for continuous flowering; divide every six to ten years in late autumn or early spring; prefers humus-rich, moist, slightly acidic soils in partial shade; USDA hardiness zones 5 through 9.

Disporum smilacinum (chigo-yuri): 20 to 25 cm (8 to 10 in) high; USDA hardiness zones 4 through 8; perennial; one or two pendent flowers on each stem in spring; in groups as underplanting; partial shade; needs consistently moist soil that does not dry out nor becomes too wet.

Eupatorium fortunei (fuji-bakama): 1 m (3 ft 3 in); USDA hardiness zones 4 through 9; moist soil; pale lavender umbels in autumn.

Filipendula purpurea (kyoganoko): 1.2 m x 60 cm (4 ft x 2 ft); USDA hardiness zones 3 through 8; forms clumps of toothed leaves and feathery crimson flowers in summer; full sun to partial shade; good by water.

Gentiana makinoi (oyama-rindo): USDA hardiness zones 5 through 9; herbaceous perennial; pale blue flowers in late summer; acid soil; plant between rocks.

Gymnaster savatieri (gymnaster/ Aster savatieri; miyako-wasure): pale blue or white aster-like flowers in September and October; good for underplanting; full sun or partial shade; height 30 to 60cm (1 to 2ft), spreading 60 to 75cm (2 to 2½ft); USDA hardiness zones 5 through 7.

Heloniopsis orientalis (shojo-bakama): an evergreen perennial with strap-like leaves forming a

flatish rosette; star-shaped flowers produced at the end of flower spikes in the spring; prefers shade; USDA hardiness zones 5 through 8.

Hemerocallis spp. *Hemerocallis fulva* (tawny daylily; kanzo/wasure-gusa) is native to eastern Asia, but has escaped from cultivation in much of North America and become invasive; many garden cultivars are available; *H. fulva* "Kwanso" (yabu-kanzo) is the naturally occurring tawny daylily with double flowers; *H. lilioasphodelus* (manshu-kisuge) is a dainty yellow daylily and a parent of many garden selections; USDA hardiness zones 4 through 9.

Hepatica nobilis var. *japonica* (yuki-wari-so): USDA hardiness zones 5 through 8; neutral, heavy soil in partial shade; a semi-evergreen perennial; star-shaped purple-blue flowers in early spring, often before leaves appear; resents being transplanted; also good for rock gardens.

Iris japonica (shaga): USDA hardiness zones 7 through 9; frost hardy; flowers in spring to early summer; well-shaded, moist soil.

Iris sanguinea (ayame): a beardless iris with grass-like leaves, bearing violet flowers on stems in late spring; moist but not wet soil in full sun; height to 90cm (3ft); USDA hardiness zones 4 through 9.

Liriope muscari (yabu-ran): USDA hardiness zones 5 through 10 (requires a sheltered spot in zone 5); an evergreen perennial; produces pale lavender flower-spikes in autumn; clump-forming; well-drained soil in sun, partial shade or shade; *L. spicata* (ko-yabu-ran), which has lavender to white flowers in late summer, spreads aggressively and is difficult to eradicate once established; tolerant of drought; can be used as ground-cover.

Millettia japonica (false dwarf wisteria; hime-fuji): a species of legume with narrow wisteria-like leaves; produces long shoots which should be pruned back to create a dense shrub; violet flowers in the summer in Japan; rich, moist soil; can be grown in a container and is often used for bonsai work; will grow to 60 to 90cm (2 to 3ft) in height; USDA hardiness zone 8; hardy to -12°C/10°F (half hardy if grown in a container).

Physalis alkekengi (Chinese lantern; hozuki): USDA hardiness zones 3 through 9; a hardy perennial; sun; grown for bright orange, papery, lantern-shaped seed pods in autumn; can spread agressively by its rhizomes, so plant in a container.

Platycodon grandiflorus (balloon flower; kikyo): USDA hardiness zones 3 through 8; purple (sometimes white or pink) flowers in early autumn, sometimes in summer; sunny, rich soil; flower-buds like tiny paper balloons before opening.

Polygonatum falcatum (fragrant Solomon's seal; naruko-yuri): USDA hardiness zones 4 through 8; greenish-white delicate pendulous flowers along stem in late spring and early summer.

Sedum alboroseum (syn. *Hylotelephium erythrostictum*; autumn stonecrop; benkei-so): "Mediovariegatum" has leaves with yellow to creamy white splashes; large, white flower heads in late summer; full sun to partial shade; well-drained soil; height to 50cm (20in) with a 30 to 45cm (12 to18in) spread; USDA hardiness zones 4 through 9.

Sedum kamtschaticum (Russian stonecrop; kirin-so): a creeping sedum cultivated in Japan since the eighteenth century; a good ground-cover plant that is spreading in habit without being invasive; yellow flowers late summer; drought-tolerant; good drainage essential; full sun; height to about 15cm (6in); USDA hardiness zones 4 through 9; "Variegatum" has green leaves splashed cream and orangey-yellow flowers.

Saxifraga fortunei var. *incisolobata* (daimonji-so): a mound-forming herbaceous perennial found in humid, but rocky, mountainous areas of Japan, flowering from August-November; *S. fortunei* "Rubrifolia" has rounded, bronzy leaves and sprays of white flowers; *S. fortunei* "Magenta" has bronze foliage, and magenta flowers late autumn into winter; partial to full shade; regular watering necessary; to 25cm (10in) in height, spread from 20 to 50cm (8 to 20in); USDA hardiness zones 6 through 9.

Stauntonia hexaphylla (mube): an evergreen climber with glossy oval leaves and lightly scented, dainty, bell-like flowers in the spring; fruit produced if both male and female plants are present; used for pergolas; tolerant of both very acid and very alkaline soils; can grow to 9m (30ft) or more; USDA hardiness zones 8 through 11; frost hardy.

Tricyrtis hirta (toad lily; hototogisu): 60 to 100 cm (2 to 3 ft 3 in) high; USDA hardiness zones 4 through 8; a clump-forming perennial; spotted purple flowers in summer to early autumn; prefers moist, slightly acidic, well-shaded conditions; plant in clumps.

Aquatic Plants

Acorus gramineus (Japanese rush; sekisho): USDA hardiness zones 6 through 9; a semi-evergreen perennial with narrow aromatic leaves for boggy ground, damp conditions, waterside; sun to partial shade; the dwarf variety needs very little soil so long as roots remain consistently wet; can also be planted in containers with water covering the crowns; flowers in May to June; height to 30cm (12in), spreading 30cm (12in).

Iris ensata (hana-shobu): USDA hardiness zones 4 through 9; sun; keep roots moist from spring until autumn; keep dry during autumn and winter; split and repot after flowering; slightly acid aquatic soil; do not plant deep; the more fancy varieties are better suited for pot culture where the blooms can be admired close at hand; do not give too much nitrogenous fertilizer.

Iris laevigata (rabbit-ear iris; kakitsubata): USDA hardiness zones 5 through 9 and warmer areas of zone 4; prefers cooler summers; a marginal perennial; needs to have its roots wet all year round; good for a shelf in a pond.

Iris tectorum (Japanese roof iris; ichihatsu): a vigorous, clump-forming, rhizomatous iris with 30cm (12in)-long, glossy, green, strap-like leaves and crested lilac to bluish-purple flowers in the spring; good for wet areas around ponds; acid soil with organic matter; full sun to partial shade; the rhizomes and rootstock are poisonous if ingested; rootstock and seeds can also cause skin irritation; 25 to 40cm (10 to 16in) in height; USDA hardiness zones 4 through 9.

Nelumbo nucifera (sacred lotus; hasu): hardy to USDA hardiness zone 4 if the roots are not allowed to freeze; leaves up to 80 cm (2 ft 8 in) across; single or double, creamy-white or pink flowers in summer held on stalks well above leaves, up to 1.5 m (5 ft) above water level; sun; rich soil; from spring gradually increase water depth to 40 to 60 cm (1 ft 4 in to 2 ft) or 15 to 22 cm (6 to 9 in) for smaller cultivars; in frost zones, grow in containers, reduce water levels in autumn, overwinter in a frost-free place, ensuring that the rhizomes are kept moist.

Nuphar japonica (Japanese pond lily; kohone): an aquatic perennial producing round, cupped flowers, yellow tinted orange, during the summer; leaf spread to 90cm (3ft); water depth to 30cm (12in); USDA hardiness zones 5 through 9.

Nymphaea spp. (water-lilies; suiren): deciduous, aquatic perennials; popular in Japan for water basins as well as garden ponds; plant the rhizomes in a shallow flower pot and submerge in the water basin, propping up the bottom of the flower pot with another pot and adjusting the water level so that the leaves float on the surface of the water – goldfish are often added to such basins in Japan – but refresh the water regularly so it does not become stagnant; *N. tetragona* (pygmy water-lily; hitsuji-gusa), a small water-lily native to Japan as well as to large areas across north-eastern Asia, northern India, Siberia, Europe, and the northern regions of the United States, has white star-like blooms with yellow

facing page, from top left:
Skimmia japonica *"Redruth", photographed in January*
Liquidambar orientalis *in November*
Autumn colour on the oak-leaf hydrangea
(Hydrangea quercifolia)
Cornus stolonifera *"Flaviramea", photographed in December*

stamens (hardy in USDA hardiness zones 4 through 11); dwarf "Laydekeri" hybrids, in shades of red and pink, produced from this species.

Saururus chinensis (lizard's tail; hangesho): a herbaceous perennial useful for planting along pond margins and in boggy soils; if grown in containers, can tolerate water up to 15cm (6in) in depth; grows in height to 30 to 90cm (1 to 3ft), with a likewise spread; flower spikes produced June, drooping at first, then becoming upright; surface of the leaves at the very top of the plant turns white during early summer; full sun to partial shade; looks best planted en masse; USDA hardiness zones 4 through 9.

Non-traditional Alternatives

Evergreens

Arbutus unedo "Compacta": a dense, upright, evergreen shrub with whitish pink flowers from October to December; a sheltered site preferred for the attractive red berries; cinnamon-coloured bark; prune to maintain rounded shape; tolerant of alkaline soils; full sun or open shade; USDA hardiness zones 7 through 10.

Hebe cupressoides: 1.2 x 1.2 m (4 ft x 4 ft); USDA hardiness zones 7 through 9; frost hardy; cypress-like leaves; flowers early to midsummer.

Myrtus communis (common myrtle; ginbaika): 4.5 x 3 m (14 ft 6 in x 9 ft 9 in); USDA hardiness zones 9 through 11; frost hardy; dense and leafy; scented white flowers in late summer, purple-black fruits; *M. luma* is slightly larger, with flaking cinnamon-coloured bark; flowers in late summer.

Ozothamnus ledifolius: USDA hardiness zones 8 through 9; frost hardy; a shrub from Tasmania with aromatic, dark green leaves, forming a round bush; *O. thyrosoides* (snow-in-summer) grows to 3 m (9 ft 9 in) and produces white flower-heads in summer.

Ruscus aculeatus (butcher's broom; nagi-ikada): 50 cm (1 ft 8 in); USDA hardiness zones 7 through 9; male and female plants needed if red berries are wanted, unless a self-fertile variety is chosen; very shady conditions; use for underplanting and hedges.

Sarcococca confusa (sweet box): to 2 m (6 ft 7 in); a round shrub; fragrant, inconspicuous white flowers in winter; can be used as an informal hedge; shade; tolerates sun only if soil is moist; USDA hardiness zones 6 through 9.

Skimmia japonica (miyama-shikimi): 60 cm to 1.2 m (2 to 4 ft); USDA hardiness zones 6 through 9; male and female plants necessary for the bright red, winter (highly poisonous) berries; shady site with moist, well-drained, acidic soil; shares its Japanese name *shikimi* with another plant,

Illicium anisatum, the branches of which are traditionally used in Japan in Buddhist funeral rites; for this reason, *S. japonica* is not much grown in Japanese domestic gardens.

Deciduous shrubs

Fothergilla gardenii (dwarf witch alder): to 1 m (3 ft 3 in); USDA hardiness zones 5 through 9, may survive in zone 4 if in a sheltered location; a bushy shrub; fragrant flower-spikes like bottle-brushes in spring before leaves; good autumn leaf colour; fertile, moist, acid soil in full sun.

Liquidambar orientalis (oriental sweetgum): to 6 m (19 ft 6 in); USDA hardiness zones 7 through 9; full hardy to frost hardy in the UK; a slow-growing, bushy tree; good autumn colour, turning purple, orange and yellow; acid to neutral soil in sun; *L. styraciflua* "Moonbeam" grows even more slowly.

Flowering trees/shrubs

Calycanthus floridus (Carolina allspice; kurobana-robai): a dense, rounded, deciduous shrub native to the south-eastern United States; height to 1.8 to 3m (6 to10ft); scented, reddish-brown flowers with strap-shaped petals from April to July; prune immediately after flowering to maintain size and shape; USDA hardiness zones 4 through 9; *C. occidentalis* (Californian allspice/California sweetshrub) produces scented, dark-red flowers; height to 3m (10ft); USDA hardiness zones 6 through 9.

Ceanothus thyrsiflorus var. *repens* (creeping blue-blossom): a compact, evergreen shrub with sky-blue flowers in early summer; USDA hardiness zones 8 to 10; "Cynthia Postan" is a mound-forming, evergreen Californian lilac cultivar with powder-blue flowers; encourage branching in evergreen varieties of ceanothus by pinching out soft tips when the shrub is still young; when older, shrubs can be maintained in size by shortening over-long branches after flowering; *C. hearstiorum* is a very low growing, evergreen species with scented leaves and flowers, a good ground-cover plant in a suitable location, requiring part shade and some moisture in the summer; recommended for USDA hardiness zones 9 through 10; frost hardy in the UK.

Chionanthus virginicus (fringe tree; Amerika-hitotsuba-tago): a slow-growing, deciduous tree native to the eastern United States; scented feathery white flowers May to June; yellow autumn leaf colour; tolerant of air pollution; requires minimum pruning; eventual height to 3.5 to 6m (12 to 20ft) with a similar spread; USDA hardiness zones 3 through 9.

Cornus florida (flowering dogwood; hana-mizuki): first sent from the United States to Japan in 1915 in return for the Japanese cherries presented by the city of Tokyo to Washington

D.C.; has become extremely popular in Japan, especially since the 1970s, for their flower heads, foliage and autumn leaf colour; prune to shape plant in late autumn after leaf fall; USDA hardiness zones 5 through 9.

Edgeworthia chrysantha (oriental paperbush; mitsumata): a small, deciduous shrub with fanning branches; small, scented flowers, yellow fading to white, produced in round dense heads in late winter; bark traditionally used for making Japanese *washi* paper; moist, well-drained, neutral to acidic soil; up to 1.5m (5ft) in height; USDA hardiness zones 7 through 10; frost hardy.

x *Halimiocistus wintonensis* "Merrist Wood Cream": a low, spreading, evergreen rock rose bearing cream-coloured flowers with burgundy spots at the base of each petal in early summer; well-drained, sandy, poor to moderately rich soil; sun; height to 60cm (2ft), spreading to 90cm (3ft); USDA hardiness zones 7 through 10; full hardy to frost hardy.

Leycesteria formosa (Himalayan honeysuckle): 2 x 2 m (6 ft 7 in x 6 ft 7 in); USDA hardiness zone 7 and warmer areas of zone 6; full hardy to frost hardy; forms thickets; attractive white flowers with brownish-purple bracts in summer to early autumn; sun or partial shade; in colder areas mulch deeply before winter.

Syringa vulgaris (common lilac): USDA hardiness zones 5 through 9; prune back in winter when first planted to encourage bushy growth; many varieties, including those with a very compact habit, are available.

Zenobia pulverulenta (dusty zenobia; suzuran-no-ki): a compact, small to medium-sized, slow-growing, semi-deciduous shrub, native to eastern North America, with scented flowers resembling lilies-of-the-valley produced in racemes in May through to June; oval leaves dusted with a blue-grey bloom, turning colour in the autumn; prune back older, longer stems immediately after flowering; height 60 to 120cm (2 to 4ft), spreading 90 to 120cm (3 to 4ft); acidic, moist soils, good for boggy sites; autumn leaf colour best in full sun; USDA hardiness zones 5 through 9.

Winter interest

Alnus incana (grey alder); *Alnus glutinosa* (common alder): USDA hardiness zones 2 through 6; many garden varieties for wet but well-drained situations (*A. incana* will tolerate drier soils); pendulous

facing page, from top left:
Welsh poppy (Meconopsis cambrica)
Yellow flag iris (Iris pseudacorus)
Yucca gloriosa
Trillium grandiflorum

catkins and brown cone-like fruit on bare branches in late winter; handsome foliage.

Cornus alba (red-barked dogwood/tartarian dogwood): 3 x 3 m (9 ft 9 in x 9 ft 9 in); USDA hardiness zones 3 through 7; red stems in winter; prune to the ground in spring for new growth; good autumn leaf colour; good waterside shrub.

Cornus sericea (syn. *C. stolonifera*; red osier dogwood): USDA hardiness zones 3 through 10; "Midwinter Fire" produces red and yellow stems; "Winter Beauty" has striking orange branches.

Salix alba var. *vitellina* (golden willow): bright yellow to orange winter shoots; "Britzensis" has orange-red winter shoots and "Chermesina" has bright red shoots; USDA hardiness zones 2 through 9.

Salix caprea "Kilmarnock" ("Kilmarnock" willow): 1.5 to 2 m (5 ft to 6 ft 7 in); USDA hardiness zones 4 through 8; a weeping willow with grey catkins in the early spring; suitable for smaller gardens.

Viburnum grandiflorum: 2.5 x 2.5 m (8 ft x 8 ft); USDA hardiness zones 6 through 8 ; a deciduous shrub; fragrant pink-flushed flower clusters on leafless branches during winter.

"Wild" flowers

Agapanthus africanus (murasaki-kunshiran): a clump-forming perennial native to South Africa with strap-like leaves and tall flower stalks bearing clusters of white, blue or purple-blue flowers; a hard frost may cause leaves to die back; height to 60 to 90cm (2 to 3ft), spreading 60 to 120cm (2 to 4ft); USDA hardiness zones 8 through 10; half hardy.

Astrantia major (masterwort): 30 to 90 cm x 45 cm (1 to 3 ft x 1 ft 6 in); USDA hardiness zones 4 through 9; a clump-forming, hardy perennial; small, pale pink, five-petalled flowers, surrounded by white bracts, early to midsummer, sometimes later; moist, rich soil; sun or partial shade; *A. maxima* is slightly taller.

Crocosmia x crocosmiiflora (montbretia; hime-hiogi-zuisen) introduced to Japan from Europe as a garden plant by the beginning of the twentieth century, montbretias have become naturalised in parts of the country; the preference in Japan is for the cultivars with smaller, red-tinged orange flowers; USDA hardiness zones 7 through 11.

Ipheion uniflorum (spring starflower/springstar; hana-nira): a clump-forming native of South America producing drifts of strap-like leaves in the spring, and pale blue (or white) six-petalled flowers on short stalks in late winter into early spring; carpeting; USDA hardiness zones 5 through 9.

Kirengeshoma palmata (ki-renge-shoma): 60 to 120 cm (2 to 4 ft); USDA hardiness zones 5 through 8; clumps of broad leaves and slender stalks with pale yellow tubular flowers; moist, acid soil in partial shade; mulch with leaf-mould.

Meconopsis cambrica (Welsh poppy): USDA hardiness zones 6 through 10; flowers in yellow, orange or even red; grows in dry places such as the base of hedges, and seeds itself very easily; partial shade to shade.

Trillium grandiflorum: the great white trillium of North America; USDA hardiness zones 4 through 8; *T. kamtschaticum* (enrei-so): an indigenous Japanese species to about 20 cm (8 in) in height; three-petalled reddish-purple flowers in spring; moist, rich, deep, acid to neutral soil in shade; USDA hardiness zones 5 through 8.

Foliage plants

Chamaemelum nobile "Treneague" (chamomile): USDA hardiness zones 4 through 9; non-flowering variety; suitable for ground-cover.

Festuca glauca (blue fescue): USDA hardiness zones 4 through 9; an evergreen perennial grass forming dense tufts of spiky bluish-grey leaves to 20 cm (8 in) long.

Helictotrichon sempervirens (blue oat grass): USDA hardiness zones 4 through 9; a tufted grass, evergreen and perennial, with grey-blue leaves up to 25 cm (10 in) long; well-drained alkaline soil; sun.

Heuchera cylindrica (coral flower/coral bells); 30 to 50 cm x 30 cm (1 ft to 1 ft 8 in x 1 ft); USDA hardiness zones 4 through 9; a perennial for moist, rich, well-drained neutral soil; sun or partial or complete shade; round-lobed dark green leaves; creamy-coloured flowers in spring to midsummer on ends of long stems; also *H. micrantha* and several cultivars, esp. "Pewter Moon".

Phormium tenax (New Zealand flax): USDA hardiness zones 9 through 11 (may survive in zones 7 and 8 if provided with deep mulch in a sheltered location); frost hardy; a clump-forming, evergreen perennial with rigid, architectural leaves to 3 m (9 ft 9 in); many variegated cultivars.

Phuopsis stylosa: USDA hardiness zones 5 through 8; good ground-cover for dry soils; spreads slowly; pink pincushion flower-heads; *P.s.* "Purpurea" has purple flowers.

Thymus serpyllum (creeping thyme): USDA hardiness zones 4 through 8; excellent ground-cover; well-drained, poor soil in full sun or partial shade; if it begins to get straggly, prune hard before flowering.

Yucca gloriosa (Spanish dagger): 1.5 m (4 ft); USDA hardiness zones 6 through 11; an architectural plant for large gardens; needs sun and well-drained soil, especially in winter; sharp, stiff leaves and spikes of bell-shaped white flowers in late summer to autumn.

Aquatic plants

Iris pseudacorus (yellow flag): 90 cm to 1.5 m (3 to 5 ft); USDA hardiness zones 5 through 9; yellow flowers in mid to late summer; vigorous.

Iris versicolor (blue flag): 35 to 60 cm (1 ft 2 in to 2 ft); USDA hardiness zones 3 through 9; flowers early to mid-summer. *I. virginica* (southern blue flag) is slightly less hardy.

Lysichiton camtschatcensis (bog arum; mizu-basho): spreading to 75 cm (2 ft 6 in); USDA hardiness zones 5 through 7; marginal aquatic perennial; white spathes produced early in spring.

Key to Frost Hardiness Terminology

Frost tender: damage possible by temperature below 5°C/41°F

Half hardy: hardy to temperatures down to 0°C/32°F

Frost hardy: hardy to temperatures down to -5°C/23°F

facing page:
Pine trees prepared for winter in the garden at Kenroku-en, in Kanazawa, Japan. These umbrella-like bamboo struts are designed to protect the tree branches from the weight of heavy snow. Used on both trees and smaller shrubs, they are wonderfully decorative in their own right; Japanese gardens are designed to be interesting all year round.

USDA
Hardiness
Zones

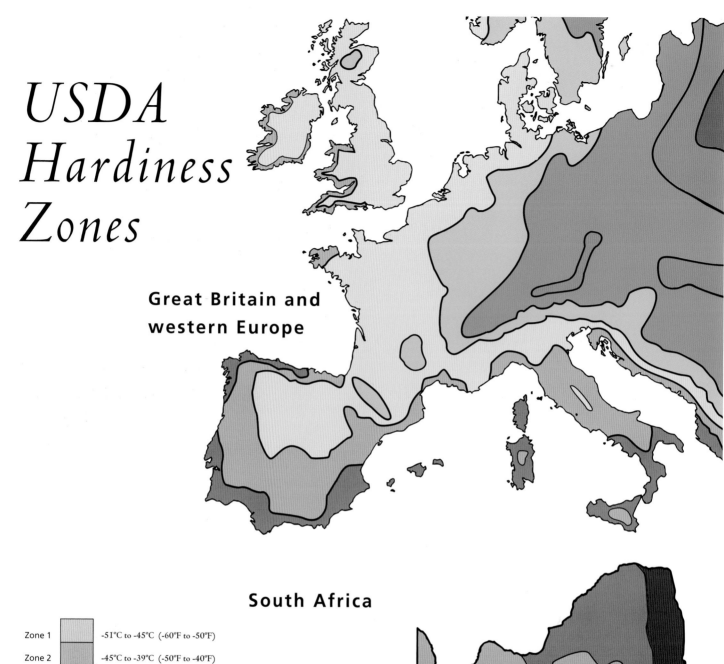

Great Britain and
western Europe

South Africa

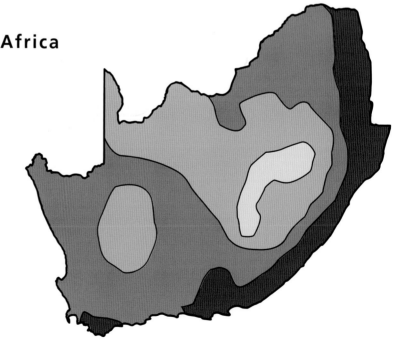

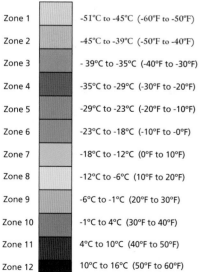

Zone 1		-51°C to -45°C (-60°F to -50°F)
Zone 2		-45°C to -39°C (-50°F to -40°F)
Zone 3		- 39°C to -35°C (-40°F to -30°F)
Zone 4		-35°C to -29°C (-30°F to -20°F)
Zone 5		-29°C to -23°C (-20°F to -10°F)
Zone 6		-23°C to -18°C (-10°F to -0°F)
Zone 7		-18°C to -12°C (0°F to 10°F)
Zone 8		-12°C to -6°C (10°F to 20°F)
Zone 9		-6°C to -1°C (20°F to 30°F)
Zone 10		-1°C to 4°C (30°F to 40°F)
Zone 11		4°C to 10°C (40°F to 50°F)
Zone 12		10°C to 16°C (50°F to 60°F)

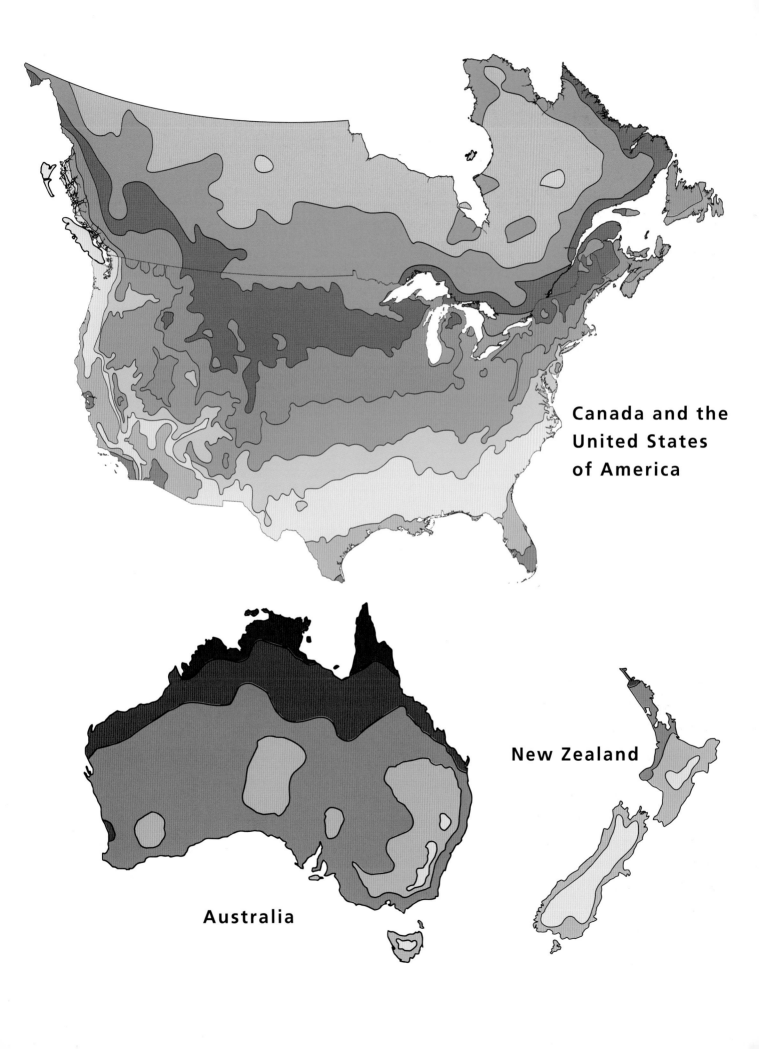

**Canada and the
United States
of America**

New Zealand

Australia

Bibliography

Aoki, Koichiro. *Edo no engei* [Gardening in Edo]. Tokyo: Chikuma Shobo, 1998.

Bessatsu Taiyo. *Kyo no koniwa* [Small Gardens of Kyoto] 78 (Summer 1992).

Brown, Kendall H. *Quiet Beauty: The Japanese Gardens of North America.* Photographs by David M. Cobb. Tokyo and Rutland, VT: Tuttle Publishing, 2013.

Cave, Philip. *Creating Japanese Gardens.* London: Aurum Press, 1993.

Conder, Josiah. *Landscape Gardening in Japan.* Yokohama: Kelly & Walsh, 1893.

Davidson, A. K. *The Art of Zen Gardens: A Guide to their Creation and Enjoyment.* Los Angeles: Jeremy P. Tarcher, 1983.

Du Cane, Florence. *The Flowers and Gardens of Japan.* London: Adam and Charles Black, 1908.

Engel, David H. *A Thousand Mountains, A Million Hills: Creating the Rock Work of Japanese Gardens.* Tokyo: Shufu-no-tomo-sha/Japan Publications, 1995.

Funakoshi, Ryoji. *Hanaki niwaki no seishi sentei* [Maintaining and Pruning Flowering and Garden Trees]. Tokyo: Shufu-no-tomo-sha, 1990.

Glattstein, Judy. *Enhance Your Garden with Japanese Plants: A Practical Source Book.* New York: Kodansha, 1996.

Hobson, Jake. *Niwaki: Pruning, Training and Shaping Trees the Japanese Way.* Portland, OR: Timber Press, 2007.

Japanese Garden Society of Oregon, with Kate Jerome. *Oriental Gardening.* New York: Pantheon Books, 1996.

Kanto, Shigemori. *The Japanese Courtyard Garden: Landscapes for Small Spaces.* Trans. Pamela Pasti. New York and Tokyo: Weatherhill, 1981. (Originally published as *Kyoto tsubo niwa* [Courtyard Gardens of Kyoto]. Kyoto: Mitsumura-suiko-shoin, 1980.)

Katagiri, Keiko. *Juki* [Trees]. Photography by Yoichiro Kaneda. Tokyo: Seito-sha, 1996.

Kawarada, Kunihiko (ed.). *Rakuyoju joryokuju no seishi to sentei* [Training and pruning deciduous and evergreen trees]. Tokyo: Nagaoka Shoten, 2013.

Keane, Marc P. *Japanese Garden Design.* Rutland, Vermont and Tokyo: Charles E. Tuttle, 1996.

Kodansha editorial staff. *Kurashi o tanoshimu niwaki no hon* [Trees to make your life enjoyable]. Tokyo: Kodansha, 2014

Kunishige, Masaaki and Funakoshi, Ryoji (eds). *Niwaki Hanaki* [Garden and Flowering Trees]. Tokyo: Nippon Hoso Shuppan Kyokai, 1991.

Masaki, Satoru. *Nachuraru gaden: jumoku zukan* [Trees for a natural-style garden]. Tokyo: Kodansha, 2012.

Mitford, Algernon Bertram Freeman-, 1st Baron Redesdale. *The Bamboo Garden.* London: Macmillan, 1896.

Mitsuhashi, Kazuo and Takahashi, Ichiro. *Wagaya no niwazukuri* [Creating Gardens at Home]. Tokyo: Shufu-to-seikatsu-sha, 1984.

Miyamoto, Kenji. *Nihonteien no Mikata* [Looking at Japanese Gardens]. Kyoto: Gakugei Shuppan, 1998.

Mizuno, Katsuhiko. *Kyoto hana no meitei sanpo* [A Stroll Through the Famous Flower Gardens of Kyoto]. Tokyo: Kodansha, 1997.

Nippon Zoen Kumiai Rengo (ed.). *Niwaki no sentei: kotsu to tabu* [Pruning Garden Trees: Practical Hints and Taboos]. Tokyo: Kodansha, 1996.

Nitschke, Günter. *Japanese Gardens: Right Angle and Natural Form.* Berlin: Benedikt Taschen, 1993.

Ohashi, Haruzo (photographer). *Chatei: The Tea Garden.* Tokyo: Graphic-sha, 1989.

Ohashi, Haruzo (photographer). *The Indoor Garden.* Tokyo: Graphic-sha, 1987.

Okada, Fumio. *Mini teien tsukuri kotsu no kotsu* [Creating miniature gardens]. Tokyo: Rural Cultural Assoc. Japan, 1993.

Ono, Masaaki (ed.). *Tsuboniwa no susume* [Creating Courtyard Gardens]. Tokyo: Kodansha, 1994.

Oster, Maggie. *Japanese Garden Style: Eastern Traditions in Western Garden Design.* London: Cassell, 1993.

Saito, Katsuo and Wada, Sadaji. *Magic of Trees and Stones: Secrets of Japanese Gardening.* New York: Japan Publications, 1964.

Seike, Kiyoshi and Kudo, Masanobu. *A Japanese Touch for your Garden.* Tokyo: Kodansha, 1995.

Shirahata, Yozaburo. *Daimyoteien* [Daimyo Gardens]. Tokyo: Kodansha, 1997.

Tanaka, Seidai. *Nippon no teien* [Gardens of Japan]. Tokyo: Kashima Shuppankai, 1967.

Tatsui Teien Kenkyusho (ed.). *Karesansui no hanashi* [About Dry-Landscape Gardens]. Tokyo: Kenchiku-shiryo-kenkyusha, 1991.

Tatsui Teien Kenkyusho (ed.). *Suikinkutsu no hanashi* [About Musical Water Features]. Tokyo: Kenchiku-shiryo-kenkyusha, 1990.

Tatsui Teien Kenkyusho (ed.). *Takegaki no hanashi* [About Bamboo Fences]. Tokyo: Kenchiku-shiryo-kenkyusha, 1990.

Yoshikawa, Isao. *Japanese Stone Gardens: Appreciation and Creation.* Tokyo: Graphic-sha, 1992.

Yoshikawa, Isao. *Puro ni manabu takegakizukuri* [Learning How to Make Bamboo Fences the Professional Way]. Tokyo: Graphic-sha, 1997.

Yoshikawa, Isao. *Takegaki no dezain* [Bamboo Fence Designs]. Tokyo: Graphic-sha, 1988.

Gardens to visit

UNITED KINGDOM

Batsford Park, Moreton-in-Marsh, Gloucs, Tel: 01386 701441

Broughton House, High Street, Kirkcudbright, Dumfries and Galloway, Tel: 01557 330437

Compton Acres, Canford Cliffs Rd, Poole, Dorset, Tel: 01202 700778

Harthill and Calderstones Botanic Gardens, Liverpool

Heale Gardens, Middle Woodford, Salisbury, Wiltshire, Tel: 01722 782504

Iford Manor, Bradford-on-Avon, Wiltshire, Tel: 01225 863146

Japanese Garden, Irish National Stud, Tully, Kildare, Tel: 0045 521617

Japanese Garden and Landscape, Kew (Royal Botanic Gardens), Richmond, Surrey, Tel: 020 8332 5655

Kildrummy Castle Gardens, Alford, Aberdeenshire, Tel: 01975 571203

Kyoto Garden, Holland Park, London

Mount Ephraim, Hernhill, Faversham, Kent, Tel: 01227 751496

Tatton Park, Knutsford, Cheshire, Tel: 01625 374400

Torosay Castle Gardens, Craignure, Isle of Mull, Argyll and Bute, Tel: special garden opening days, contact 077389 33033

Zen Garden, St Mungo Museum of Religious Life and Art, Glasgow, Tel: 0141 276 1625

NORTH AMERICA

Anderson Japanese Gardens, Rockford, IL, Tel: 815-229-9390

The Bloedel Reserve, Bainbridge Island, WA, Tel: 206-842-7631

Brooklyn Botanic Garden, Brooklyn, NY, Tel: 718-623-7200

Fort Worth Botanic Garden, Fort Worth, TX, Tel: 817-392-5510

Garvan Woodland Gardens, Univ. of Arkansas, Hot Springs, AK, Tel: 501-262-9300

Hakone Estate and Gardens, Saratoga, CA, Tel: 408-741-4994

The Huntington Library, Art Collections and Botanical Gardens, San Marino, CA, Tel: 626-405-2100

Japanese Tea Garden, Golden Gate Park, San Francisco, CA, Tel: 415-752-1171

Nishinomiya Tsutakawa Japanese Garden, Manito Park, Spokane, WA

Nitobe Memorial Garden, Univ of British Columbia, Vancouver, BC, Tel: 604-822-6038

Portland Japanese Garden, Portland, OR, Tel: 503-223-1321

Roji-en, The Morikami Museum and Japanese Gardens, Delray Beach, FL, Tel: 561-495-0233

Sansho-en, Chicago Botanic Garden, Glencoe, IL, Tel: 847-835-5440

Seattle Japanese Garden, Washington Park Arboretum, Seattle, WA, Tel: 206-684-4725

Seiwa-en, Missouri Botanical Garden, St Louis, MO, Tel: 314-577-5100

Shofuso Japanese House and Gardens, Philadelphia, PA, Tel: 215-878-5097

Suiho-en, The Donald C. Tillman Water Reclamation Plant, Van Nuys, CA, Tel: 818-756-8166

Suppliers and trade addresses

All information provided is accurate at time of printing. Some addresses serve as geographical reference only; not all suppliers have retail stores. Please call each supplier or visit their website for more information.

UNITED KINGDOM

Stones, Gravel and Sand

IMAG Ltd
1 Fountain Street
Congleton, Cheshire, CW12 4BE
Tel: 01260 278810
www.imag.co.uk

Long Rake Spar Company
Youlgrave
Nr. Bakewell
Derbyshire
DE4 1LW
Tel: +44 1629 636 210
www.longrakespar.co.uk

Lanterns, water basins, bridges, benches, bamboo fences

Bridges for Gardens
2 Croft Road
Wokingham
Berkshire RG40 3HU
Tel: 0118 9781080
www.bridgesforgardens.com

The Japanese Garden Centre
Addlestead Road
East Peckham
Kent TN12 5DP
Tel: 01622 872403
www.buildajapanesegarden.com
(A comprehensive selection of materials, including stepping stones, decorative stones, water features, bamboo fences and garden buildings)

Japan Garden
Unit 6
Bankside Industrial Estate
Ledbury HR8 2DR
Tel: 01531 630091
www.japangarden.co.uk
(A good selection of Japanese garden materials, including basins, bamboo fences, bridges, as well as garden buildings)

Plants

The Beth Chatto Gardens
Elmstead Market
Colchester
Essex CO7 7DB
Tel: 01206 822 007
www.bethchatto.co.uk

Big Plant Nursery Ltd
Hole Street
Ashington
West Sussex RH20 3DE
Tel: 01903 891466
www.bigplantnursery.co.uk
(Bamboos, Japanese maples, Gingko varieties)

Bowden Hostas
Bowdens, Cleave House, Sticklepath
Okehampton, Devon EX20 2NL
Tel: 01837 840989
www.bowdenhostas.com
(Hostas, ferns, grasses and bamboos)

Burncoose Nurseries
Gwennap, Redruth, Cornwall TR16 6BJ
Tel: 01209 860316
www.burncoose.co.uk
(Japanese trees and shrubs)

Cotswold Garden Flowers
Sands Lane
Badsey, Evesham, Worcestershire WR11 7EZ
Tel: 01386 422829
www.cgf.net
(Perennials)

Edrom Nurseries
Coldingham
Eyemouth
Berwickshire, Scotland
TD14 5TZ
Tel: 01890 771386
www.edrom-nurseries.co.uk
(Rare perennials from China and Japan)

Hardy Exotics Nursery
Gilly Lane, Whitecross, Penzance
Cornwall, TR20 8BZ
Tel: 01736 740660
www.hardyexotics.co.uk
(Exotics including *Cycas revoluta* and *Musa basjoo*)

Kelways
Picts Hill
Langport
Somerset TA10 9EZ
Tel: 01458 250521
www.kelways.co.uk
(Tree peonies)

Lilies Water Gardens
Broad Lane, Newdigate
Surrey RH5 5AT
Tel: 01306 631064
www.lilieswatergardens.co.uk

Mallet Court Nursery
Marshway, Curry Mallet
Taunton TA3 6SZ
Tel: 01823 481493
www.malletcourt.co.uk
(Trees and shrubs from China, S. Korea, Japan)

P. M. A. Plant Specialities, Junker's Nursery
Junker's Nursery Ltd, Higher Cobhay
Milverton, Somerset TA4 1NJ
Tel: 01823 400075
www.junker.co.uk
(An extensive list of Japanese trees and shrubs, including maples)

Roadford Water Gardens
Higher Goodacre Farm
Broadwoodwidger
Lifton, Devon PL16 0ER
Tel: 07790 779991
www.roadfordwatergardens.co.uk
(Aquatic and marginal plants, including *Iris ensata* and *I. laevigata*, by mail order)

Whitelea Nursery
Whitelea Lane
Tansley, Matlock
Derbyshire DE4 5FL
Tel: 01629 55010
www.uk-bamboos.co.uk
(specialist bamboo nursery)

SOUTH AFRICA

Cape Garden, Joostenbergvlakte
56 Tarentaal Rd
Joostenbergvlakte, Kraaifontein, Cape Town
Tel: 021 988 4137
www.capegardencentre.co.za
(other branches at Stellenbosch and Somerset West)

Garden Shop, Broadacres
Broadacres Lifestyle Centre, Broadacres
Tel: 0861 427336
www.gardenshop.co.za
(other branches at Bryanston, Edenvale, Boksburg, Menlo Park and Parktown North)

Tulbagh Nursery
Nooitgedacht Farm
Tulbagh Rd, Tulbagh, Western Cape
Tel: 023 230 0694
tulbaghnursery.co.za

AUSTRALIA

Imperial Gardens Landscape/Hidden Orient Shop & Nursery
208 Forest Way
Belrose, NSW 2085
Tel: 02 9986 3968
www.imperialgardens.com.au

Austral Watergardens
1295 Pacific Highway, Cowan, NSW 2081
Tel: 02 9985 7370
www.australwatergardens.com.au

Bamboo Down Under
930 Tamborine-Oxenford Rd,
Wongawallan, QLD 4210
Tel: 07 5573 1844
www.bamboodownunder.com.au

Conifer Gardens Nursery
254 Mt Dandenong Tourist (Cnr Sherbrooke Road)
Ferny Creek, VIC 3786
Tel: 03 9755 1793
www.conifer.com.au

Donnelly's Garden Supplies
2/860 Ballarto Road, Cranbourne South, VIC 3977
Tel: 03 9782 2855
www.donnellysgardensupplies.com.au

Rock & Stone
33 Tooronga Rd, Malvern East, VIC 3145
Tel: 03 9571 6266
www.rocknstone.com.au

Yamina Collectors Nursery
34 Mt Pleasant Rd, Monbulk, VIC 3793
Tel: 03 9756 6335
yaminacollectorsnursery.com.au

NEW ZEALAND

Mauways Nursery
State Hwy 1, RD 5, Hunterville, Wanganui 4785
Tel: 06 322 9863
mauways.co.nz
(online nursery)

Stone and Water World
218A Marua Rd, Mt Wellington, Auckland 1051;
343 Albany Hwy, Rosedale, Auckland 0632
Tel: 09 525 3142
stoneworld.co.nz

Wairere Nursery
826 Gordonton Rd, RD 1, Hamilton 3281
Tel: 07 824 3430
www.wairere.co.nz

NORTH AMERICA

Plants

Camellia Forest Nursery
620 Hwy 54 West, Chapel Hill, NC 27516
Tel: 919-968-0504
www.camforest.com

Fantastic Plants
5416 Hacks Cross Rd, Memphis, TN 38125
Tel: 901-387-7025
www.fantasticplants.com

Fraser's Thimble Farms
175 Arbutus Rd, Salt Spring Island, BC, V8K 1A3
Tel: 250-537-5788
www.thimblefarms.com

(rare plants including many from Japan)

The Honey Tree Nursery
24202 Hwy 2, Norboro, PEI, C0B 1M0
Tel: 902-836-2044
thehoneytreenursery.com

Lake's Nursery
8435 Crater Hill Rd, Newcastle, CA 95658
Tel: 530-885-1027
www.lakesnursery.com

Mendocino Maples Nursery
41569 Little Lake Rd, Mendocino, CA 95460
Tel: 707-397-5731
www.mendocinomaples.com

Lazy S's Farm Nursery
2360 Spotswood Trail, Barboursville, VA 22923
www.lazyssfarm.com
(mail order nursery selling rare woodland perennials, many from Japan)

Moss Acres
59 Bates Rd, Honesdale, PA 18431
Tel: 1-866-438-6677
www.mossacres.com

Mt Pleasant Iris Farm
PO Box 346, Washougal, WA 98671
Tel: 360-835-1016
www.mtpleasantiris.com

Oriental Garden Supply LLC
448 W Bloomfield Rd, Pittsford NY 14534
Tel: 585-586-3850
www.orientalgardensupply.com

RareFind Nursery
957 Patterson Rd, Jackson, NJ 08527
Tel: 732-833-0613
www.rarefindnursery.com

Shin-Boku Nursery
230 Beech Hill Rd, Wentworth NH 03282
Tel: 603-764-9993
www.shin-bokunursery.com

Springdale Water Gardens
340 Old Quarry Ln, Greenville, VA 24440
Tel: 1-800-420-5459
www.springdalewatergardens.com
(irises, water lilies, marginal and aquatic plants)

Wabi Sabi Japanese Gardens
1719 S Pines Rd, Spokane, WA 99206
Tel: 509-999-6802
www.wabisabigardens.com

Water garden
The Water Garden LLC
5212 Austin Rd, Chatanooga, TN 37343
Tel: 423-870-2838
watergarden.com

Van Ness Water Gardens
2460 N Euclid Ave, Upland, CA 91784
Tel: 800-205-2425 / 909-982-2425
www.vnwg.com

Bamboo
Bamboo Garden
18900 NW Collins Rd, North Plains, OR 97133
Tel: 503-647-2700
www.bamboogarden.com

Bamboo Plantation
709 Highway 84 W, Brookhaven, MS 39601
Tel: 601-833-5669
www.bamboogardencenter.com

Canada's Bamboo World
8450 Banford Rd, Chilliwack, BC, V2P 6H3
Tel: 604-792-9003
www.bambooworld.com

Lewis Bamboo
121 Creekview Rd, Oakman, AL 35579
Tel: 1-877-796-2263
www.lewisbamboo.com

Stone lanterns, basins and garden accents
A Oregon Decorative Rock
11050 SW Denney Rd, Beaverton, OR 97008
Tel: 503-646-9232
www.oregondecorativerock.com

Japanese Style
413 4th Ave NW, New Prague, MN 56071
Tel: 877-226-4387
www.japanesestyle.com

Noble House and Garden
6408 Lakeside Drive, Flower Mound, TX 75022
Tel: 888-430-4455
www.noblehouseandgarden.com

Northwest Landscape and Stone Supply
5883 Byrne Rd.
Burnaby, BC, V5J 3J1
Tel: 604-435-4842
www.landscapesupply.com

Pacific Stonescape
34008 Texas St, Albany, OR 97321
Tel: 541-928-7678
www.pacificstonescape.com

Stone Forest
213 S. St. Francis Drive, Santa Fe, NM 87501
Tel: 1-888-682-2987
www.stoneforest.com

Photography credits & acknowledgements

Fotolia.com: Parc Ritsurin à Takamatsu, Shikoku by LU0810 (22); Jardin zen japonais by rudiuk (43);日本庭園by Saruri (86); 八橋と杜若 (小石川後楽園) by kohashi (149br); Beautiful view of Japanese Garden by alexandros33 (151t). **Garden Picture Library:** David Askham 116-117; Mark Bolton 135tr; Philippe Bonduel 141tr; Brian Carter 147tl; Christi Carter 137tr, 139tl; Eric Crichton 147tr; John Glover 141bl, 141br, 145tl; Sunniva Harte 147br; Neil Holmes 137tl; Lamontagne 117r, 135tl, 139br; John Neubauer 135bl; Joanne Pavia 43; Howard Rice 137bl, 145tr, 145br; Gary Rogers 114; JS Sira 143tl; Ron Sutherland 16, 60, 130-131, 132-133; Juliette Wade 145bl; Rachel White 3. **Jerry Harpur:** 11, 13r, 18-19, 21, 25, 26, 31, 34, 37, 38, 39, 49, 59, 68-69, 75tr, 75bl, 76, 77, 79, 80, 86, 89, 92-93, 95, 103, 106, 110, 113, 118, 119, 120, 124; des. MP Keane 61, 62-63; des. Jeff Mendoza 40; Mrs Pomeroy, CA 46, 66, 72, 75tl; 102; Terry Welch 9, 105. **Sunniva Harte:** 1, 20, 28, 36, 47, 56, 94, 96, 97. **Anne Hyde:** 14. **JTB Photo Library:** 24. **Marc Peter Keane:** 48. **Andrew Lawson:** 22, 70-71, 73, 82, 108, 115, 121. **Marianne Majerus:** des. Peter Chan and Brenda Sacoor 27, 42, 91. **Kazuo Mitsuhashi:** 87, 109, 112. **Clive Nichols:** 6-7, 12-13, 15, 84-85, 139tr; des. Richard Coward 100; des. Dowle & K Ninomiya 4, 98; des. Robert Ketchell & Eileen Tunnell 129. **Katsutoshi Okada:** 32-33, 50-51, 55, 58. **Photos Horticultural:** 135br, 137br, 139bl, 141tl, 143tr, 143bl, 143br, 147bl. **David Scott:** 44, 75br. **Shutterstock.com:** Wisteria in April in Tokyo by Masami Reilly (122); spike winter hazel by Inomoto (139tl); Lizard's tail, Saururus chinensis by shihina (143bl); An Image of Iris Garden by KPG_Payless (149t); Magnolia flowers by terimma (151b). **Tony Stone Images:** David Ball 8. **Patrick Taylor:** 123. **Pamla Toler:** des. Paul Sheppard 64, 65 (des. Paul Sheppard, K. Wood). **Elizabeth Whiting & Associates:** 45, 52, 104. **Isao Yoshikawa:** 125, 126, 127.

I am grateful to New Holland Publishers (UK), who published the original edition of this book as *Serene Gardens*, for having given me the opportunity to write on a subject that is very close to my heart. The designer Grahame Dudley and illustrator Sandra Pond helped to make the book visually exciting as well as informative. My editor, the late Sandra Raphael, made sure I did not fall short of her exacting standards, while Yvonne McFarlane at New Holland deftly steered the entire project through to its completion.

I wish to thank Fox Chapel Publishing for undertaking this new enlarged edition of the book, which has allowed me to augment various chapters with new material which will hopefully help to deepen the reader's interest in and appreciation of the Japanese approach to gardens. My editor, Colleen Dorsey, and her team at Fox Chapel have been meticulous in their attention to detail, and I am deeply grateful to them for their patience and expertise.

I would like to express my gratitude to my parents, to my literary agents, Mike and Alice Sharland, and above all to my husband, Simon Rees, for his unwavering support and encouragement.

Published 2016—IMM Lifestyle Books
www.IMMLifestyleBooks.com

IMM Lifestyle Books are distributed in the UK by Grantham Book Service, Trent Road, Grantham, Lincolnshire, NG31 7XQ.

In North America, IMM Lifestyle Books are distributed by Fox Chapel Publishing, 1970 Broad Street, East Petersburg, PA 17520, www.FoxChapelPublishing.com

Copyright © 2000, 2016 by IMM Lifestyle Books
Copyright © 2000, 2016 in text Yoko Kawaguchi
Copyright © 2000, 2016 in photography see photography credits

ISBN 978-1-5048-0004-4

Printed in Singapore
10 9 8 7 6 5 4 3 2 1

General index

Note: Page numbers in *italics* include photo/illustration captions.

Index of plants